# A WOMAN'S GUIDE TO SPIRITUAL WARFARE

# A Woman's Guide to Spiritual Warfare

*A Woman's Guide for Battle*

by Quin Sherrer
and
Ruthanne Garlock

**Regal**

**From Gospel Light**
**Ventura, California, U.S.A.**

PUBLISHED BY REGAL BOOKS
FROM GOSPEL LIGHT
VENTURA, CALIFORNIA, U.S.A.
PRINTED IN THE U.S.A.

Regal Books is a ministry of Gospel Light, a Christian publisher dedicated to serving the local church. We believe God's vision for Gospel Light is to provide church leaders with biblical, user-friendly materials that will help them evangelize, disciple and minister to children, youth and families.

It is our prayer that this Regal book will help you discover biblical truth for your own life and help you meet the needs of others. May God richly bless you.

*For a free catalog of resources from Regal Books/Gospel Light, please call your Christian supplier or contact us at* 1-800-4-GOSPEL *or* www.regalbooks.com.

Cover and illustration by Charles Piccirilli and Bob Coe

**Library of Congress Cataloging-in-Publication Data
(Applied for)**

ISBN: 0-8307-3518-6

1  2  3  4  5  6  7  8  9  10  11  12  13  14  15  /  10  09  08  07  06  05  04

Rights for publishing this book in other languages are contracted by Gospel Light Worldwide, the international nonprofit ministry of Gospel Light. Gospel Light Worldwide also provides publishing and technical assistance to international publishers dedicated to producing Sunday School and Vacation Bible School curricula and books in the languages of the world. For additional information, visit www.gospellightworldwide.org; write to Gospel Light Worldwide, P.O. Box 3875, Ventura, CA 93006; or send an e-mail to info@gospellightworldwide.org.

## OTHER BOOKS BY THE AUTHORS

*How to Pray for Your Children*
Quin Sherrer

*How to Forgive Your Children*
Quin Sherrer with
Ruthanne Garlock

*How to Pray for Your Family and Friends*
Quin Sherrer with
Ruthanne Garlock

*Before We Kill and Eat You*
Ruthanne Garlock

*Fire in His Bones*
Ruthanne Garlock

# Contents

# Acknowledgments

THANKS TO ALL THOSE who joined in praying for us while this project was underway. Thanks also to all the women who willingly allowed us to share their stories—defeats as well as victories. Without your transparency, our job would have been impossible.

To our husbands, John Garlock and LeRoy Sherrer, a special thank you for giving us the time and freedom to write this within our deadline.

Appreciation also to Servant's editor, Beth Feia, for her prayer support, encouragement, and editing.

Special gratitude and love to

the Lord Jesus Christ,
our Commander-in-Chief,

who calls us, equips us, and goes ahead of us into battle.

# Introduction

"WOMEN WARRIORS—SHARING THE DANGER." The magazine headline grabbed my attention as I stood at the airport newsstand checkout. A determined-looking military police-woman in full battle gear stared at me from the cover.

Only the day before I'd spoken with Beth Feia of Servant Publications and agreed to coauthor *A Woman's Guide to Spiritual Warfare*. The analogy was striking. A crisis in the Persian Gulf, triggered by a power-hungry, egocentric villain had prompted the greatest rallying of military strength the United States had seen since World War II. Journalists called Saddam Hussein "the thief of Baghdad who stole a country."

"If only Christians could recognize it, the crisis in the spiritual realm is far greater than this threat of war," I mused while reading the magazine during my flight. "And the spiritual battle we are in is also triggered by a power-hungry, egocentric villain—Satan himself. He's trying to steal not just a country, but the whole earth."

When I first started teaching on spiritual warfare more than ten years ago, I often got quizzical looks from women who seemed unaware that a spiritual battle was going on. Now I get mostly knowing nods. Many women are eager to learn how to be more effective in fighting their battles against discouragement, fear, harassment, and other ploys of the evil one.

Here's what some women experience:

> LeAnn balances her crying baby on one hip while getting breakfast for her husband and two school-age children. "Lord," she prays, "it's so hard being a mother. What am I doing wrong?"
>
> Madeline suspects her husband is seeing another woman. Her children are grown. Madeline feels bored and useless. She wonders, "Lord, is there more to life than this?"
>
> Ora Mae sits in a recliner chair and daydreams about her childhood. "Lord," she prays, "I don't see what purpose you have for me now."

Quin and I don't claim to be experts on the subject of spiritual warfare. Yet we have gained some knowledge through independent research and study, and through encounters "in the trenches." This book is an accumulation of our combined experience and of testimonies from women just like you who are learning to be skilled warriors.

Sure, men are also called to duty, but women have a special interest in this battle. After all, our involvement in the war began with the woman and the serpent in the Garden of Eden. And it's the seed of the woman—Jesus—who has bruised the head of the serpent and secured his defeat.

Jesus has done everything necessary to ensure our victory over Satan, but that doesn't mean it's a walkover. Yes, Jesus came to set the captives free, but all the prisoners haven't yet heard the good news. So we must be faithful to the call to spiritual battle.

Our purpose is best expressed by the motto adopted by Moravian missionaries to the Caribbean in the 1700s: "To gain for the Lamb the reward of his sacrifice."

War is expensive. It requires money, energy—even lives. The same is true for spiritual warfare. But to have a part in the ultimate victory—and to hear Jesus say, "Well done, good and faithful servant"—is worth any hardship we endure in the battle.

—Ruthanne Garlock

# ONE

# But I Never Wanted to Be in a Battle!

*For our struggle is not against flesh and blood, but against the rulers, against the authorities, against the powers of this dark world and against the spiritual forces of evil in the heavenly realms.* **Ephesians 6:12**

"I RESIST YOU IN THE NAME OF JESUS and command you to go!" Claudia said with a quavering voice. To her amazement, the hideous black leopard turned and ran. Startled, she awoke from the bad dream and sat up in bed.

"I realized the Lord was teaching me in my dream to do spiritual warfare—that the name of Jesus really has power," shared this trim brunette. "I had accepted Jesus as my Savior and Lord, and had received the Holy Spirit. But then my mind was bombarded with fear and condemnation. I loved God more than anything, yet the enemy made me think I had blasphemed the Holy Spirit and would never be able to please God."

Claudia had never received any teaching on how to deal

with fear. She had heard some comments about "spiritual warfare," but she had no clue as to what that meant. She thought she simply had to endure this struggle in exchange for her salvation. Then she had her dream.

"In the dream I was constantly being pursued by a huge black leopard. I pushed it out the door and it came in the window. Everywhere I went it followed me. I was terrified. Then I felt the Lord say to me, 'Claudia, resist the leopard in the name of Jesus.' In my dream I stopped running, turned and faced the leopard, and commanded it to leave in Jesus' name. I was happily surprised to see it flee!"

Claudia's friend Jean took her to a woman who ministers in deliverance, because there was witchcraft in Claudia's family background, and she had used drugs in college. The Lord broke these and many related bondages.

Jean became Claudia's prayer partner and began to train her in scriptural truths. "Now," Claudia says, "I know a Christian can truly be victorious over the spiritual forces of evil that Paul talks about in Ephesians."


## DO WE NEED TO FIGHT THE DEVIL?

My subject was prayer. My audience, three dozen pastors' wives. I had been asked to teach a weekend workshop at a rustic lodge hidden away in the Georgia pines. But after the first session, in which I briefly discussed spiritual warfare, the leader who had invited me knocked on my door.

"Quin, you've offended some of our women here," she said apologetically. "Several of them have Ph.D.'s, and they don't believe Christians need to fight the devil in our day and age. Please tone down your message."

I'd only shared some basic guidelines on intercession and how to pray the Word of God as a means of opposing the enemy. Then I had explained that Satan—not another person—is our enemy, and we need to be on guard against his tactics. I was stunned to think a group of pastors' wives would find such teaching offensive. But I agreed to adapt my material.

The apostle Paul's many references to spiritual warfare clearly indicate that he considered warring against the powers of darkness to be normal activity for Christians.But my experience at the retreat offers a graphic example of a common attitude among many Christians today.

"Spiritual warfare? Those two words don't go together!" a friend exclaimed upon hearing of plans for this book.

"Don't you even believe the devil exists?" we might ask these people.

Well, yes, they do—"theologically speaking." But the tendency is to think of Satan not as a personality or a being who affects us directly, but simply as a pervasive influence of evil in the world.

"There are two equal and opposite errors into which our race can fall about the devils," writes C.S. Lewis. "One is to disbelieve in their existence. The other is to believe, and to feel an excessive and unhealthy interest in them."[1]

Some of the pastors' wives at that retreat had apparently fallen into the first error. They either didn't believe in Satan's existence, or they mistakenly felt there was nothing they should be doing about it.

"Maybe the next time one of these women faces a direct

attack from the enemy in her life, she'll think about what I said," I told my prayer partner at the retreat.

"Well, you gave them the Word of God," my friend assured me. "And his Word never returns void."

The next afternoon as we were packing my car to leave, a young pastor's wife ran up to me.

"I just want you to know that your first lesson really opened my eyes," she said exuberantly. "I'm going home to apply some of those spiritual warfare methods, and I know things are going to change! I now realize my rebellious teenage son is not the enemy. I intend to use Scripture as a weapon to fight the devil, just as you showed us."

## A WARFARE HANDBOOK

You will find this book to be a practical handbook aimed at helping women understand the *why* and the *how* of spiritual warfare, based on biblical examples and contemporary experiences. In these pages we will address such questions as:

- What is "spiritual warfare"?
- Who is the enemy, and who started the war?
- Is warfare only for specialists?
- Is there a cost to ignoring this war?
- Is there a scriptural mandate for spiritual warfare?
- What weapons are we to use?
- Is every mishap from Satan?
- If Jesus won the victory, why do we have to fight?

- Isn't it enough simply to pray and leave the outcome in God's hands?
- What about the battle in the mind?
- How can we distinguish between God's voice and the enemy's voice?
- What should we do when we become battle-weary?
- How is Satan working in women's lives today?
- How do we become vulnerable to his work?
- How can we feel secure against his attacks?

As we share answers to these questions and recount experiences to illustrate them, you will gain insight and confidence about fighting your own spiritual battles. Also, you'll be able to encourage and strengthen a friend who may be suffering an enemy attack.

Why a spiritual warfare book for women? We believe spiritual warfare is of special interest to women for these reasons:

- Women tend to be more sensitive to the spiritual realm than men—including the area of occult activity. This sensitivity should be guided by the Holy Spirit.
- Women can become competent spiritual warriors—especially for those they love—because of their loyalty in relationships.
- Today's women face unique difficulties that need to be addressed in the context of spiritual warfare: single parenting, careers, the "Super Mom" syndrome, the influence of the media, coping with addicted children and spouses, abortion, cultural pressures of a materi-

alistic society; the list goes on.

- We feel these problems can be better addressed by prayer and waging spiritual warfare against Satan's schemes, rather than by relying solely on protests or demonstrations to achieve social and political change.

## DEBORAH'S EXAMPLE

The biblical Deborah challenges us to lay aside some of our own worthy interests and activities to deal with the spiritual battles at hand.

We read of Deborah, a prophetess and judge in Israel, in the fourth chapter of Judges. She held court under a palm tree between Bethel and Ramah at a time when Israel was suffering bitter oppression under Jabin, a Canaanite king who had defeated Israel and occupied its land.

The name *Jabin* means "cunning," and the Canaanite word comes from a root word meaning "to humiliate or bring under subjection." Deborah must have heard daily reports of Jabin's cruel treatment. His army general, Sisera, constantly terrorized the people with his nine hundred chariots of iron, while Israel's army had almost no weapons for their defense. No doubt Deborah became increasingly incensed over the situation and joined the Israelite people in crying out to the Lord for deliverance.

We modern Deborahs need to feel that same indignation about Satan's work. By prayer and spiritual warfare, we can take a stand against the enemy's oppression in our own world.

The enemy works in many ways today—some more subtle

than others. It seems his iron chariots come in all sizes! Perhaps you recognize yourself in one or more of these everyday attacks, which a friend calls "household sins":

- Strife and disharmony too often disrupt your family relationships.
- Someone you love has been unjustly treated by another Christian; you take up the defense and find yourself becoming bitter and cynical.
- Your anger seems to erupt at the slightest provocation.
- You suffer with guilt because you don't feel you're a very successful Christian.
- You struggle with envy when comparing your own circumstances with your friends' seemingly carefree lives.
- Insecurity and anxiety over the future frequently overwhelm you.
- Your prayer life is inconsistent, and you often feel that your prayers bounce back in your face.

## BUT I DON'T WANT TO FIGHT!

A friend once said to me, "Quin, I never wanted to have to fight the devil. I just wanted to remain a normal Christian, go to church, mind my own business, and not cause trouble!" But when her son got into drugs, she learned spiritual warfare out of necessity.

Thousands of women feel they've just been tending to "business as usual," trying their best to live a good Christian life. Suddenly an iron chariot comes roaring through their household, church, business, or community, thrusting them into confrontation with the enemy. And they cry out, "Help!"

You may be facing a battle similar to the ones that women have shared with us:

- Your pregnant, unwed daughter is convinced that getting an abortion is the answer to her dilemma.
- You learn your child is on drugs, and the "dealer" has been attending the church youth group.
- You discover a cache of pornographic literature in your husband's closet.
- A child threatens or attempts suicide after hearing about a classmate who killed himself.
- A teenage acquaintance confides that she was sexually abused by her father, who is a deacon in the church.
- Your church is broken into and vandalized by Satan worshipers.
- An adult porn shop opens in your neighborhood, and local authorities seem totally indifferent.
- Your Christian teenager goes into rebellion, gets caught up in rock music, and runs away from home to join a Satanist group.
- Your colleague at work divorces her abusive husband, then moves in with an older woman who is a lesbian.
- A widow you and your husband befriended convinces him that it is God's will for him to divorce you and marry her.

Such situations actually confront many Christian women today—women whose eyes are opening to the spiritual battle they are already in, even though they feel unprepared. No longer do they need to be persuaded that a war is on. They are looking for guidance as to how to fight the battle!

## DEBORAH ACTED ON GOD'S PROMISE

We can learn more from Deborah about how to deal with spiritual enemies. After suffering twenty long years of Jabin's oppression, the people of Israel began to beseech God for deliverance. He responded by instructing Deborah to say to Barak, the general of Israel's army: "The LORD, the God of Israel, commands you: 'Go take with you ten thousand men of Naphtali and Zebulun and lead the way to Mount Tabor. I will lure Sisera, the commander of Jabin's army, with his chariots and his troops to the Kishon River and give him into your hands'" (Jgs 4:6-7).

Barak, who had faced this formidable enemy before, was fearful—and with good cause. A weak volunteer army with no chariots and few weapons was no match for Sisera's well-trained army of a hundred thousand men.[2]

But Barak was assessing the situation strictly from a logistics point of view. Facts and truth are not always the same! The truth was that God had promised victory in spite of the odds, if Israel would obey him. Deborah—who was called "a mother in Israel" (Jgs 5:7)—was willing to stake the nation's future on that promise. What courage it took to give such bold instructions to Israel's army general! But she acted on God's truth, not on circumstantial facts.

Barak agreed to go, but only if Deborah went with him. After all, she was the one with the word from God. So, to see her people liberated, Deborah assumed the role of a military commander to accompany Barak in leading the troops to battle. It was a necessary but unpleasant task (see Jgs 4:8-10).

## GOD'S STRATEGY

Deborah received specific orders from God about the placement of Israel's troops. They were to march to Mount Tabor. As they approached the Kishon River, Sisera received intelligence reports as to Israel's movements. He gathered his army and went out against Israel, unaware that he was actually cooperating with God's plan.

This was the greatest display of Sisera's military might Barak and Deborah had ever seen. He had mobilized all his soldiers, weapons, and chariots to annihilate Israel's weak army. Barak, surveying the situation from his vantage point on the mountain, may have had second thoughts about going against Sisera. But Deborah was not deterred by this show of strength. She knew it was Sisera's *last* show!

As Sisera's army came close to the Kishon River, Bible scholars suggest that God caused a freak rainstorm, which blinded the soldiers and caused the river to flood, sweeping the iron chariots downstream (see Jgs 5:4, 20-22). The name *Kishon* is from a root word meaning "to ensnare."

Scripture records the outcome: "Then Deborah said to Barak, 'Go! This is the day the LORD has given Sisera into your hands. Has not the LORD gone ahead of you?' So Barak went down Mount Tabor, followed by ten thousand men. At Barak's advance, the LORD routed Sisera and all his chariots and army by the sword, and Sisera abandoned his chariot and fled on foot.... All the troops of Sisera fell by the sword; not a man was left" (Jgs 4:14-16).

One version of the text says, "Then the Lord threw the enemy into a panic,... not one man was left alive" (Jgs 4:15-16, *TLB*).

Sisera took refuge in the tent of Jael, a Canaanite woman whom he thought he could trust. But Jael, choosing to align herself with the people of God, was not content to be a passive bystander in this war. Using household tools at hand—a mallet and a tent stake—she killed the enemy commander. End of Sisera. End of those dreaded iron chariots.

Amazing, isn't it? Two women were the key players in this drama, in which God enabled a weak army, outnumbered ten to one, to win a resounding victory. Seven penetrating words end the story: "Then the land had peace forty years" (Jgs 5:31).

## DEBORAH'S KEYS TO VICTORY

Deborah and Barak were assured of victory because they battled according to God's instructions. God would not do it for them without their effort, nor did he reveal the entire strategy in advance. They had to obey God without knowing all the reasons why. God determined the place of the battle and told them how many soldiers to take. Deborah and Barak obeyed; God responded by intervening with the "impossible."

These same principles apply in the spiritual battles we

face. Final success *is* assured, but we have to seek God's direction and put forth some effort. When we use Deborah's seven keys to victory in assaulting the enemy's iron chariots, we too can see our enemy defeated.

1. She recognized it was a *spiritual* battle, and that God was going ahead of her small army.
2. She obeyed God's instructions, trusting his strategy.
3. She did not focus on the seeming strength of the enemy.
4. She did not waver in her confidence in God's Word.
5. She refused to be deterred by her colleague's lack of spiritual vision.
6. She never compromised with the enemy.
7. She gave praise and glory to God for the victory.

## RUTHANNE DOES BATTLE

I remember the day an enemy "iron chariot" rolled through my family. I received word that my younger brother Jerry, then a missionary in Belgium, had cancer of the throat. An inoperable tumor, the doctors said. My emotions ran the gamut of shock, anguish, despair, then anger.

Family members and friends on both sides of the Atlantic began to pray, asking God to intervene. I thought it significant that the enemy had hit his throat, trying to prevent him from preaching the gospel. So I began to bind the spiritual powers that were attacking him.

Two different intercessors, one in Texas and one in

Belgium, each received a word from the Lord for Jerry from John 11:4: "This sickness is not unto death, but for the glory of God, that the Son of God might be glorified thereby" (*KJV*).

As we prayed over the next several months, we stood on that promise. Jerry underwent painful interferon treatments and radiation therapy, and he was forced to take medical leave from his missions assignment. But he began to improve. Nine months later all tests showed the tumor was gone, and doctors could find no signs of cancer in his body.

For almost eight years he was free of cancer. Then one morning in 1989 he discovered a lump under his chin. Tests showed a malignant tumor in his throat, in the same spot where the previous tumor had been.

Again I became angry at the enemy. "I choose to believe that God hasn't changed his mind since he said eight years ago this sickness is not unto death!" I wrote in a letter to my brother. "I feel the same anger I used to feel when I ran off the neighborhood bullies who tried to beat you up after school. The enemy is just trying to bully you, and we have to take a stand against him!"

The recurrence of cancer came soon after Jerry had taken a pastorate in Missouri, and the congregation there mobilized a twenty-four-hour prayer chain. His Christian doctor accompanied him to Texas to consult with specialists at a cancer treatment center.

For months Jerry flew back and forth to Texas for chemotherapy and radiation treatments. While we knew that the Great Physician was in charge of his case, we also recognized that it was a physical *and* spiritual battle.

During that time two different friends—whom I hadn't even known during Jerry's first illness—told me they felt led to exhort me and my family to stand on John 11:4. That confirmation greatly encouraged us.

Jerry required a shorter course of treatment than specialists had first planned. After a few months, tests showed the tumor was gone. He also surprised his doctors with the level of activity he was able to maintain.

Now, just as this book is being completed, I've received word that an inoperable tumor is growing behind Jerry's right eye. He is again embarking on a treatment program.

My first reaction was tears and grief, but I went to a friend for prayer and we entered into warfare. I decided to take off my crying clothes and put on my fighting clothes! We are putting our confidence in God and his Word, not in the specialists' prognosis. Once again we are applying Deborah's keys to victory, and we expect God's Word to prevail.

We really don't have a choice. The battle is on. And if we're sold out to Jesus, we're in it.

A woman's place is in the war! We recognize, as Deborah did, that God has gone ahead of us. And as Claudia discovered, we have authority in the name of Jesus.

Now let's take a closer look at our enemy.

# TWO

# Who Is the Enemy? And What Does He Want from Me?

*So the LORD said to the serpent, "... I will put enmity between you and the woman, and between your offspring and hers; he will crush your head, and you will strike his heel."* **Genesis 3:14-15**

SATAN IS OUR ARCHENEMY. Scripture clearly confirms that he's the foe of every human being, starting with Adam and Eve. The name *Satan* actually means "adversary, or one who opposes." Yet any discussion about warfare with this enemy tends to repel many believers.

"Satan, demons, evil principalities and powers—these are scary things that frighten people," some Christians say. "It's just too spooky!"

But to ignore this enemy and hope he will ignore us is both unrealistic and hazardous.

Arthur Mathews says:

The terrifying fact of a hostile world of evil and malicious spirits paralyzes many Christians into inactivity and un-willingness to seek out biblical answers and to apply them.... There are many clear indications of Satan's mo-tives and methods given us in the Bible, if only we would heed them.... His central purpose is to pull God from His throne in the minds of men and to take that throne him-self."[1]

## WHY SATAN HATES YOU AND ME

Ever since God created Adam and Eve and placed them in the Garden of Eden, Satan has had a special hostility toward women. This fallen archangel, fuming with anger toward God and his creatures, lurked about the garden looking for a place where he could get a foothold and break the loving re-lationship between God and human beings.

Pride and rebellion led to Satan's own fall from heaven. Ultimately he induced Eve to succumb to those same sins. The serpent and the daughters of Eve have been at enmity ever since. Satan not only hated Eve; he hates all her off-spring—including you and me.

This hatred was expressed centuries ago by the sacrifice of children to evil gods. Then at Jesus' birth, through King Herod's order to kill all the babies under age two, Satan tried to murder the Messiah. He failed. Later he engineered Jesus' crucifixion and thought he'd won at last. Actually, that was Satan's biggest mistake. Jesus' sacrificial death, burial, and resurrection fulfilled the Father's plan to atone for sin and nullify Satan's plan. Scripture declares: "The reason the Son of God appeared was to destroy the devil's work" (1 Jn 3:8).

Godly women remain a frustration to Satan. Think about it! Women bring human beings into the world, and Satan hates humans. He still tries to do away with them through child sacrifice, abortion, and sexual sin.

## BLOCKING THE MESSAGE

Jesus completed the work the Father gave him to do on earth, and the enemy can do nothing to change that perfect plan of salvation. But Satan *does* keep people from hearing the message; he also distorts and misrepresents the message. In other words, he vents his rage against the Father by taking vengeance on us. Satan tries to prevent our deliverance and keep us alienated from God, knowing this frustrates God's desire to see us reconciled to himself.

Paul explains it: "If our gospel is veiled, it is veiled to those who are perishing. The god of this age has blinded the minds of unbelievers, so that they cannot see the light of the gospel of the glory of Christ, who is the image of God" (2 Cor 4:3-4).

We then must oppose the spirits of darkness which blind and deceive the minds of the hearers. We must also resist evil forces trying to hinder our reaching people with the gospel. Our goal is to see men and women—believers and unbelievers—set free from the bondage of Satan by the power of the blood of Jesus.

Bible teacher Dean Sherman makes the point that God and Satan are not equally powerful forces standing in opposition to one another. Satan is merely a created being, while

God is "the great uncreated Creator."[2]

Speaking of Satan's attempt to exalt himself and become like God, Sherman says: "What Satan did was absolutely ludicrous. Yet we, as finite, puny beings... think we can run our own lives without God. To try to live without God is to try to be God. This is exactly the absurd and insane pride that entered Satan's heart, and sadly, we all have it.

"... The being called Satan is merely a fallen archangel who received his name because he opposed God. He is also our adversary. We must consider him to be that—no more and no less."[3]

## BINDING THE LIE OF SATAN

Sue, a former student, called one day and asked Ruthanne to pray for her unsaved father who had terminal cancer. Sue and her mother had prayed for years for him to accept Jesus. Now near death, he was very bitter, blaming God for his illness.

"How can we lead him to Christ when he is so angry?" Sue asked me.

"The problem is, he's believing Satan's lie that God is his enemy," I responded. "He needs to see that God is his only source of help. I suggest you bind the lying spirit that has deceived him. Then just shower your father with unconditional love; don't preach to him anymore."

Sue's mother and brother picked up extension phones, and I prayed while they agreed: "Thank you, Father, that it is your desire to bring Sue's dad into your kingdom. We take authority in the name of Jesus and bind the deceiving spirits that are lying to him. We ask the Holy Spirit to reveal the truth that you love him. Lord, cause him to come to his senses and escape from the trap of the devil. We ask this in Jesus' name, Amen."

I suggested they continue this strategy. "Use the authority Jesus gave you to forbid the enemy to speak to your father."

About six weeks later Sue called to tell me her father had died. But just before he died, he received Jesus as his Lord.

"One day as I walked through the living room where he was lying on the sofa, I went over and hugged him and said, 'I love you, Dad,'" Sue related. "Tears came to his eyes—it was the first time I had ever seen him cry. As I began to share with him about the Lord, I could tell the Holy Spirit had already prepared his heart. He willingly accepted Jesus right then!"

This is a classic case of a person being deceived by evil spirits to believe God is his enemy. But his eyes were opened to the truth when spiritual warfare was done on his behalf. Realizing God truly was his friend, he repented.

## HOW DOES SATAN WORK?

We find in Scripture many names attributed to Satan, which reveal both his methods and his character. He is called

- crafty (Gn 3:1)
- the deceiver (Gn 3:13)
- the foe and the avenger (Ps 8:2)
- the destroyer (Is 54:16)
- the tempter (Mt 4:3; 1 Thes 3:5)

- ruler of demons [Beelzebub] (Mt 12:24)
- a murderer (Jn 8:44)
- a liar and the father of lies (Jn 8:44)
- the evil one (Mt 6:13; Jn 17:15)
- god of this age (2 Cor 4:4)
- an angel of light (2 Cor 11:14)
- the ruler of the kingdom of the air (Eph 2:2)
- the dragon,... that ancient serpent (Rv 12:7-9)
- the accuser (Rv 12:10).

Journalist and author McCandlish Phillips deftly describes the way Satan operates:

Consider the tactics of an enemy in battle. The enemy finds it far easier to send death upon his target if he conceals and hides his own position, so that he may strike by sudden surprise. Sneak attack, it is called. To obtain this advantage, the enemy moves in darkness, by stealth, and takes his position of advantage over the target in a hidden or camouflaged place. He wants the other side to be as unalert as possible, unguarded, unsuspecting, exposed to attack. The enemy will also use deceit and trickery to create a false impression of what and where the dangers are. The less the intended victims know of his existence, his position, his intention, and his power, the greater the advantage to him in bringing injury or death upon them.

These are the tactics of Satan toward man. The less you know about Satan, the better he likes it. Your ignorance of his tactics confers an advantage upon him, but he prefers that you do not even credit his existence. If you do not believe that he is, then you will do nothing to prepare yourself, or your family, or your children, against his activities, and by that neglect many are made his victims.[4]

## THE ENEMY'S ADVANTAGE

Several years ago I accompanied my husband, John Garlock, on a ministry trip to Guatemala. One day our host took us to the ancient city of Antigua to visit an historical museum. This region had once been inhabited by the Mayan Indians, but the Spanish conquered the area in the early 1500s. A huge mural in the museum depicts the conflict.

The Mayan Indians—who fought with bow and arrow—were known to be brave, fierce warriors. But the Spanish soldiers had a distinct advantage because they wore armor, and they had horses and guns. Horses were unknown in the Western Hemisphere at that time. So when the Indians saw one of these swift-footed beings with an armored soldier attached, they thought it was all one creature.

They aimed at the horse, not realizing that the real enemy was the soldier astride the horse. Their arrows felled the horses in great numbers, but the armored soldiers jumped from their mounts and shot the Indians with their muskets. The Mayans were massacred by the hundreds, and the Spanish easily seized control of the entire region.

"What a great illustration for spiritual warfare!" I exclaimed to my husband as we looked at the wall-to-wall painting. "The Indians were defeated because they failed to recognize the real enemy riding on the horse's back—and that's exactly what happens to countless Christians. They shoot at one another instead of fighting the devil."

"Well, then," John responded, "when another person confronts us with meanness and malice, we'd better remind ourselves, 'He's not the enemy; he's only the horse!'" Perhaps a laughable analogy, but graphic nonetheless.

In many instances Satan does his work unhindered simply because Christians are impassive or too preoccupied to take notice. Edith Schaeffer says:

There is a deafness, blindness, insensitivity of touch and feeling among many Christians who refuse to recognize the war in which *they* are involved, and who are spiritually "playing a violin" while the enemy attacks and scores victories unchallenged, given no resistance.... We are as stupid and negligent as any of the "Neros" who ever lived, if we simply entertain ourselves with Christian diversions and let ourselves and our children be attacked and devoured without entering into the army and setting up the defense we have been instructed to prepare.[5]

## SATAN DESTROYS HOMES

One of the ways the enemy attacks women is by destroying their marriages, thus causing their children to grow up in a one-parent home. Psychologist Richard Dobbins reviews the damage Satan has done in this area:

Out of the materialism of the 1950s, the narcissism of the 1960s, and the hedonism of the 1970s has risen a society that aborts its unborn, commercializes the care of its children, and warehouses its elderly. Blinded by such confused priorities, we are dehumanizing our country and destroying our family relationships.

... Millions of broken families lie strewn across our land by a flagrant disregard for the sanctity of marriage and by selfishly sought divorces. Divorced mothers and their children comprise the largest group falling below the poverty line each year. Rising numbers of children in father-absent families are crippled in their search for a heterosexual identity.... "[6]

## ONE OF THE CASUALTIES

Rena, a pastor's daughter who grew up in church, fought hard for her thirteen-year marriage to Jack, her high-school sweetheart. She even resigned her position as minister of music at their church because he felt threatened by her being in the public eye. But he was "in love" with a nineteen-year-old girl working for him, and wanted a divorce.

"I was an emotional mess. I never dreamed our ideal marriage could crumble," she explained. "When problems developed, I tried to pray. My two boys needed a daddy, and I needed a husband. But I realized I really didn't know how to pray. I knew all the Bible stories, but I had no grasp of the principles in the Word, and certainly no knowledge of the enemy.

"I remember teaching a Bible study on Mary and Martha, and realizing that with all my church work I was a Martha. I prayed earnestly, 'God, I really want to know you more.' I had no idea what I would go through as he answered that prayer.

"I could do nothing to persuade Jack to change his mind. He wanted a 'quickie' divorce, but I refused. It was two years before the divorce was granted. In the end his drinking and lifestyle led to the loss of his business, and he didn't even marry the girl he'd had the affair with.

"A counselor told me that because Jack's father drank, was unfaithful to his wife, and left when Jack was eleven, he had a compulsion to be like him. Maybe that is so. I only know my two boys went through deep hurt and rejection as we tried to begin life again in a city hundreds of miles away."

For years Rena cried over her own loss, struggling with feelings of helplessness. "I think most churches are ill-equipped to help divorced partners recover," she said, "especially those who didn't choose the divorce. When a woman's security is taken away, her self-esteem stripped, she feels like a rape victim. Suddenly she must find a job and fill the emotional needs of children who miss the other parent. She's in an almost impossible position.

"Without the Lord's help I wouldn't have made it. He put a person here and a person there to pray for me and give me helpful books. I learned to pray the Word over my family, and I learned the value of praise. Sitting at the piano I would play and sing to the Lord, and it was very healing."

Today, eight years later, Rena is completely free of guilt and bitterness. She lives with her sons on the campus of a Bible college, where she teaches music.

"God continues to answer my prayer to know him more," she said with a smile. "And my boys are being healed and are learning to know him too. He has given us joy and peace in ways I couldn't have dreamed possible."

## CLAIMING THE PROMISED LAND

We can compare our experiences in spiritual warfare with those of the children of Israel when God told them to go in and possess Canaan. They found heathen tribes in the Promised Land. God instructed them to drive out the tribes, and he promised to help them win their battles as long as they obeyed him (see Jos 23:6-13).

But, sad to say, Israel did not obey God. They compromised with their enemies, intermarried with the Canaanite tribes, and took up idol worship and other heathen practices. The tribes they should have driven out became snares for them, and they never fully possessed their Promised Land. In the end they were taken into captivity.

Just as Israel had to fight enemy tribes to possess the land, so Christians today must fight. The difference is, Israel fought flesh-and-blood enemies, while our struggle is against principalities and powers of the unseen world (see Eph 6:12).

Many Christians hold the notion that once they are believers covered by the blood of Jesus, they are immune to the enemy's influence. True, Jesus' blood cleanses us from all sin. And because we belong to him, we have authority over all the power of the enemy (see Lk 10:19; Eph 1:22). But we still have the freedom of choice. At any time we can choose *not* to obey God and *not* to avail ourselves of the power of the blood of Jesus. That wrong choice makes us vulnerable to the enemy.

Another factor to consider is that we are members of a fallen race. Our basic human weaknesses make us susceptible to the enemy's activity. Though God's great power far exceeds the power of Satan, we humans are no match for the devil if we're operating in our own strength.

More than three hundred years ago Puritan pastor William Gurnall wrote this advice:

> If you are going to take shelter under this attribute [God's almighty power], you must stay within its shade. What good will the shadow of a mighty rock do if we sit in the open sun? That is to say, if we wander away from God's protection by venturing into the heat of temptation, we should not be surprised when our faith grows faint and we stumble and fall into sin. We are weak in ourselves; our strength lies in the rock of God's almightiness. It should be our constant habitation.[7]

It is important to avoid these two extremes: first, blaming the devil for everything that goes wrong, when it could be a result of our own weaknesses or poor choices; second, not recognizing when Satan and his cohorts are at work against us or our loved ones, and failing to take authority over them.

To the degree we choose to walk in our own selfish ways instead of submitting to God's plan and purpose, we allow the enemy to gain a foothold in our lives. Thus Scripture admonishes us: "In your anger do not sin... do not give the devil a foothold" (Eph 4:26, 27). "Be self-controlled and alert. Your enemy the devil prowls around like a roaring lion looking for someone to devour. Resist him, standing firm in the faith" (1 Pt 5:8).

Paul shares his experiences of spiritual warfare: "I have fought the good fight, I have finished the race, I have kept the faith.... Demas, because he loved this world, has deserted me" (2 Tm 4:7, 10).

## FIGHTING A BATTLE ON TWO FRONTS

The enemy's attempt to draw us into sin causes our inner conflict. But if we choose to obey God, he gives us success in these skirmishes. Then we are empowered to battle outwardly, dispelling the powers of darkness and setting other captives free. The apostle Paul said he disciplined his body so that sins of his flesh would not cause him to lose that inner battle and be disqualified from doing the Lord's work (see 1 Cor 9:26-27).

We see tragic consequences today in the lives of those who fail to follow Paul's counsel:

- A Bible school graduate goes back to her old group of friends, and soon she is hooked on drugs again.
- A former missionary leaves his wife and children to become a leader in a New Age group.
- A prominent preacher sternly condemns sin (while winning many converts to the Lord), then confesses to being addicted to pornography.
- A lawyer with a twenty-year record as an excellent Christian businessman is caught embezzling two hundred thousand dollars from the local school board.

Despite these people's exploits for God, they lost the inner contest. They walked out from under the sheltering rock of

God's almighty power. Of course the Father's mercy allows for them to be restored and healed. But how much better "to be made new in the attitude of your minds" (Eph 4:23) and to walk in mastery over these struggles.

God has provided all we need to defeat this adversary of ours—both the enemy within and the enemy without. We have the "full armor of God" (Eph 6:11), and weapons with "divine power to demolish strongholds" (2 Cor 10:4).

We women *can* triumph if we choose to employ God's provision and obey his instructions. In the next chapter we will examine the specially designed spiritual wardrobe and weaponry God has prepared for us.

# THREE

# What Our Spiritual Wardrobe Should Look Like

*Therefore put on the complete armor of God, so that you may be able to stand your ground in the evil day, and, having fought to the end, to remain victors on the field. Stand therefore, first fastening round you the girdle of truth and putting on the breastplate of uprightness as well as the shoes of the gospel of peace—a firm foundation for your feet. And besides all these take the great shield of faith, on which you will be able to quench all the flaming darts of the Wicked One; and receive the helmet of salvation, and the sword of the Spirit which is the word of God. Pray with unceasing prayer and entreaty at all times in the Spirit, and be always on the alert to seize opportunities for doing so.* **Ephesians 6:13-18, Weymouth**

THESE VERSES ARE Paul's battle handbook for the churches he had founded. He wanted to prepare them for the persecution and adversity he knew would come. His writings are still the "basic training" passages for our own spiritual conflicts today.

William Gurnall, a seventeenth-century scholar, wrote:

> It is not left to everyone's fancy to bring whatever weapons he pleases; this would only breed chaos.... Look closely at the label to see whether the armor you wear is the workmanship of God or not. There are many imitations on the market nowadays.... Do not dare to call anything the armor of God which does not glorify him and defend you against the power of Satan![1]

The armor God provides is for our *defense* against evil powers; he also provides *offensive* weapons. Our warfare wardrobe is complete in every detail. But it is our responsibility to put it on and to use it.

## THE GIRDLE OF TRUTH

The girdle Paul refers to was actually a wide metal or leather belt worn by a soldier around his lower trunk to hold his armor tightly against his body and to support his sword. It was also used to carry money and other valuables. To "gird up your loins" was to prepare for action (see 1 Sm 25:13, *KJV*).

The truth is the very essence of the gospel: God's plan to free us from sin's bondage through his Son's sacrificial death, burial, and resurrection. Jesus said, "Then you will know the truth, and the truth will set you free" (Jn 8:32).

"If a person's understanding is clear in its hold on truth

and his will is sincerely grounded in holy purposes, then he is a maturing Christian," wrote Gurnall. He warns that Satan, as a serpent, assails the truth by sending false teachers who sow error. Or as a lion, he sends persecutors who threaten danger or death in trying to force the believer to deny the truth.[2]

Satan first assaulted the truth in the garden when he asked Eve, "Did God really say... ?" (Gn 3:1). Not having the belt of truth for armor, she wavered and began to doubt what God had said. Our enemy still uses this subtle weapon of doubt against us. It is "the truth that is in Jesus" (Eph 4:21) that we must fasten on tightly to protect us from the strategies of the evil one.

Nell's belt of truth slipped when she became fascinated with New Age holistic health and diets. Though she had a Christian upbringing, it wasn't long before she was in a New Age cult.

Her mother, visiting from out of state and discovering the deception, confronted the young man who had lured Nell into the cult group. She told him, "My daughter once made a commitment to the Lord Jesus Christ, and she *will* come back to him and forsake all this garbage you have exposed her to. By the power and authority of the blood of Jesus, I bind every influence of Satan you have over my daughter."

When Nell heard about the bad scene, she told her mom, "I want to live my own life, so you and Dad back off my case."

"Honey, we love you too much to let the devil keep you in his clutches," her mother responded. "We'll battle Satan with everything that's in us until the god of this world stops blinding you, and your will is freed to return to Jesus."

Nell's parents did spiritual warfare every day, telling Satan to loose her. They asked God to place a hedge of protection around her and bring to her remembrance all the truth she'd learned as a young girl. They praised the Lord for being a covenant-keeping God to those who love him and keep his commandments. They enlisted friends in both states to pray.

One day Nell wandered into a Christian bookstore to buy some health food cookbooks. "As I was leaving, the store owner insisted I buy a little book, so I did just to get him to leave me alone," she reported. "Later that night I flipped through it and noticed it was full of Scripture verses. The author suggested reading those verses three times a day, like you would take vitamins. I was into anything that would make me healthier, so I did it. Before long those Scripture verses became more important to me than any of the cookbooks or the teachings of the cult."

Five months from the time her parents began spiritual warfare for Nell, she called and asked if she could move home and start life over again with Jesus. She's since graduated from a Bible school and has ministered in several countries.

"How easy it was to get deceived when I stopped going to church, praying every day, and reading my Bible," she admits. "But thank God, my eyes were opened to the truth."

## THE BREASTPLATE OF RIGHTEOUSNESS

This piece of armor (today's equivalent is the bullet-proof vest) protects the heart and other vital organs of the soldier. The girdle or belt of truth holds it in place. *Righteousness* simply means "right action," "uprightness", or "conformity to the will of God."[3] It is important to remember that truth and righteousness always go together.

"Keep your heart with all vigilance... for out of it flow the springs of life," advised Solomon (Prv 4:23, *TAB*). Satan often tempts us to compromise our standard of righteousness with the argument, "But it's for a good cause."

Gurnall writes:

> Head knowledge of the things of Christ is not enough; this following Christ is primarily a matter of the heart.... If you are a serious soldier, do not flirt with any of your desires that are beneath Christ and heaven. They will play the harlot and steal your heart.[4]
>
> Righteousness and holiness are God's protection to defend the believer's conscience from all wounds inflicted by sin.... Your holiness is what the devil wants to steal from you.... He will allow a man to have anything, or be anything, rather than be truly and powerfully holy.[5]

Ruth left her government job because she heard God's call to full-time mission work. But when she arrived on the field, she found that her senior missionary was misusing funds. Ruth's dilemma: should she quietly excuse this behavior, or should she stand for principle and risk her friendships, her own credibility, and her work in the missions? Ruth did the latter for one big reason: she wanted to please God more than man.

"I was shocked to discover how the devil will work through weak Christians," she said. "It was a very difficult time. Some of my friends thought I was just getting into a power struggle. But I knew that to compromise on this issue to please people would mean displeasing God. Nothing is worth that. I left that group but continued working in missions, and God met all my needs. The Lord helped me to forgive that woman, and then I 'locked it out with love' so the enemy couldn't keep bringing the struggle back."

The enemy knows exactly the area where you are vulnerable to compromise in a job situation, in a friendship, in your church or prayer group, in your family relationships. He will make it seem very logical and in your own and others' best interests for you to bend your principles a bit.

Speaking to believers, James wrote, "Wash your hands, you sinners, and purify your hearts, you double-minded" (Jas 4:8). The compromising hearts of his people were God's greatest grief (see Heb 3:10). But the soldier who always has his breastplate of righteousness firmly in place, secured by the belt of truth, will be protected from a divided heart.


## THE GOSPEL SHOES OF PEACE

Putting on one's shoes is a symbol of readiness. In Paul's day shoes weren't worn indoors (and still aren't in Eastern cultures). To put on your shoes indicated you were going outside the protection of the house. God told his people to eat the Passover with their shoes on so they would be ready to flee Egypt (see Ex 12:11). The soldier's shoes protected his feet, and sometimes were fitted with metal cleats to make him more sure-footed in combat.

Again we share Gurnall's wisdom:

The peace which the gospel brings to the heart makes a saint ready to wade through any trouble that might meet him in his Christian course.... Only Christ can make a shoe fit the Christian's foot so he can easily walk a hard path, because He lines it with the peace of the gospel.... The most important provision Christ made for His disciples was not to leave them a quiet world to live in, but to arm them against a volatile and troublesome world.[6]

Joyce's shoes of peace enabled her to walk serenely through the "mine field" of her husband's wrath.

During a visit to her parents' home, Joyce and Barry were alone in the house one day when he went to take a shower. Because Joyce was running the washing machine, Barry got a burst of cold water that threw him into an unreasonable rage. Forgetting that the bathroom door was ajar and that Joyce was within earshot, he began screaming curses at her and calling her names. It was a gush of profanity that seemed demonic.

Joyce immediately began calling on God, asking, "Lord, how do I handle this?" She went to the living room and began running the vacuum cleaner while she prayed and bound the spirits of hatred and rage.

"I felt the Lord told me, 'Walk in the opposite spirit.' Barry was operating in a spirit of hate and condemnation; I needed to operate in a spirit of love and forgiveness. I forgave Barry for the cutting things he had said. By the time he came out of the bathroom, I truly had received God's peace."

As Barry was leaving to go wash his car, Joyce offered to go along and help. "I cleaned all the windows on his car, inside and out, and he had no clue that he had upset me. When we got back to the house, I confronted him with what I had heard. I was able to stand my ground and do it calmly. He didn't apologize or express any regret whatsoever. He just glared at me and said, 'I didn't know you heard,' and walked away. That experience showed me just how hardened his heart had become, but it also showed me that God's peace can sustain me no matter what happens."

Scripture assures us, "And the peace of God, which transcends all understanding, will guard your hearts and your minds in Christ Jesus" (Phil 4:7).

## THE SHIELD OF FAITH

Various kinds of shields were in use in Paul's day, but this analogy refers to the large rectangular shield that could protect the entire body. It was common practice for the soldier to "anoint" his shield with oil so it would reflect the sun's rays and blind the enemy, and also deflect his blows. Gurnall gives this insight concerning the shield:

The apostle compares faith to a shield because... the shield is intended for the defense of the whole body.... And if the shield was not large enough to cover every part at once, the skillful soldier could turn it this way or that way, to stop the swords or the arrows, no matter where they were directed.... Not only does the shield defend the whole body, but it defends the soldier's other armor also.... Every grace derives its safety from faith; each one lies secure under the shadow of faith.[7]

It is important that we have faith in God—not faith in faith. Our confidence in God must be based on his character and trustworthiness, not on our own ability to follow a formula. Scripture tells us, "Without faith it is impossible to please God, because anyone who comes to him must believe that he exists and that he rewards those who earnestly seek him" (Heb 11:6).

Because of growing up in a dysfunctional family and suffering abuse as a child, Chris was tormented with thoughts of suicide, even after she became a Christian. Through prayer and counseling the oppression lifted, and she was free.

"Then I learned that the enemy always tests your deliverance," she said. "Though I knew the Holy Spirit had powerfully ministered to me, I would occasionally have thoughts of suicide again. I had to use the shield of faith to deflect those fiery darts. Over and over I would say to the enemy, 'Satan, I resist you. I *have* been delivered in Jesus' name. I will live and not die. You are defeated, and I command you to flee.' I persisted until the enemy finally stopped bothering me in that area. I am totally free."

Simply put, faith means believing that God is who he says he is and that he will do what he says he will do. Gurnall's slogan sums it up: "He who has God's heart does not lack for His arm."[8]


## THE HELMET OF SALVATION

The helmet not only protected the soldier's head in battle; it bore insignia or symbols identifying which army he belonged to. In 1 Thessalonians 5:8 Paul instructed, "Let us be self-controlled, putting on... the hope of salvation as a helmet." This hope of salvation protects the Christian against attacks on his mind, one of Satan's primary targets.

To deal with such an attack we must learn to distinguish the voice of our enemy from God's voice. God will speak words of love, comfort, conviction, and guidance. The enemy speaks words of fear, accusation, and condemnation. Gwen's story is an example of repelling Satan's attack on the mind.

Gwen, her husband, and their thirteen-year-old grandson Mark (whom they had adopted) were in their van heading home after a holiday visit to relatives. What had been a wonderful visit had gone sour just as they were saying their goodbyes. Mark had been playing outdoors with his young cousins, one of whom got slightly hurt in a moment of Mark's carelessness. The child's mother gave Mark a tongue-lashing and embarrassed him in front of everyone.

The three of them got into the van with sagging spirits to begin their eight-hundred-mile journey in miserable silence. Mark slumped on the seat as far back in the van as he could get. As they rode along, Gwen glanced out her window and saw a reflection of herself in the glass. In her mind she heard a voice say, "You're old and fat and ugly." Studying the image for a moment she thought to herself, "It's true, Gwen. You are old and fat and ugly."

But suddenly she had a flash of insight. "That's a spirit of rejection! It came in with Mark, and it will stay with us all the way home if I permit it to," she thought.

"I immediately bound the spirit of rejection and commanded it to flee, and then prayed quietly," she reported. "In a very short time the whole atmosphere inside the van changed. Mark clambered up to the front seat and began laughing and talking with us, and we enjoyed the trip home together. Had I not resisted that attack against my mind, I would have played right into the enemy's hand."

Dean Sherman's analogy is helpful:

Every military post has guards. They stand quietly at their posts until they hear a rustling in the bushes. Then they immediately ask: "Who goes there?" and are prepared to evict any intruder. We too need to post a guard at the gate of our minds to check the credentials of every thought and every imagination, ready to cast down that which is not true, not righteous, or not of God. If it doesn't belong, out it goes. This is spiritual warfare: being alert to every thought.[9]

## THE SWORD OF THE SPIRIT

The sword is used not only to defend against the enemy, but to offensively attack him. Paul's sword is the Word of God—the *rhema*. W.E. Vine says:

The significance of *rhema* (as distinct from *logos*) is exemplified in the injunction to take "the sword of the Spirit, which is the word of God" (Eph 6:17); here the reference is not to the whole Bible as such, but to the individual Scripture which the Spirit brings to our remembrance for use in time of need, a prerequisite being the regular storing of the mind with Scripture.[10]

Lynn used the sword of the Spirit to repel a physical assault. As she was getting ready for bed one night while her husband Jay took the babysitter home, she felt an urge to pray, not knowing why. "Lord, what is this I'm feeling?" she asked. "Show me how to pray."

"Pray against a spirit of harassment," came that still, small voice. She prayed accordingly, and when she felt somewhat relieved she got into bed. In a few minutes she heard voices coming up the stairs. "Who is Jay bringing home with him at this hour?" she wondered.

The next thing she knew, a strange man knelt beside her bed with a pistol pressed to her neck. His companion, holding Jay at gunpoint, ripped out the phone cord. "Just do as he says, Lynn," Jay said quietly, "and everything will be all right."

"Give me your rings," commanded the thief as he began trying to pull them off her finger.

Forgetting Jay's advice, Lynn answered, "No! In Jesus' name, you can't have my wedding rings!"

"Then his hands drew near to touch my body," she said. "Thoughts of rape, blood, and even death entered my mind. As quickly as those thoughts came, Scriptures flowed into my heart. Although I was shaking, the promises of God filled my spirit, and total peace flooded my being. Repeatedly the man drew near, and it was as if an invisible force prevented him from going any further.

"I lay in bed crying softly with the gun still pointed to my throat, marveling that my two small children and baby were sleeping soundly and that my emotions hadn't carried me into a screaming, terrified frenzy. The other burglar went through the house gathering whatever he thought had any value. After what seemed forever, the man backed away from my bedside, left the room, and closed the door.

"Jay and I waited for some time, then crept out to survey what was left of our plundered home. To our surprise, we found all our belongings piled on the living room floor. Only a few pieces of jewelry were missing.

"Did God send some noise to scare them away? Did they see an angel? The mystery remains. But my husband had established the habit of praying aloud every time we left our house or car, 'Lord, please station your angels to guard and protect our belongings.' God proved to us, once again, that he alone is our security."

## WIELDING THE SWORD

Josette had opportunity to use the sword as an offensive weapon. When her son Troy began having difficulty with his boss on his new job, he called home for prayer. Using Scriptures from Daniel, Josette began to pray for him. "Father, may Troy find favor and compassion with his boss. May he be well-informed, quick to understand, and qualified for the job.... May he be found ten times better than others" (Dn 1:9, 4, 20).

"Satan, I block your tactics with the Word of God. My son is a mighty man of valor! God promises him prosperity. I bind spirits of pride and jealousy in his boss that are coming against Troy. You will not hinder God's plan for him on this job.

"Thank you, Lord, that Troy will be your representative on this job, and that he is becoming the man of God you created him to be."

Josette continued praying in this way as the Lord gave her

additional Scriptures. The situation gradually improved. Fourteen months later, when Troy was promoted to a job in another city, his boss gave him a farewell party and bragged about how qualified and well-informed Troy was in his work—a specific answer to his mother's prayers!

As many people's experiences attest, the Word of God is not only a sword, a spiritual weapon. It is a source of great comfort. Arthur Mathews presents a challenge:

> If we accept the fact that our role in life is that of soldiers, then we must drop our toys and become more acquainted with the weapons of our warfare. In a conflict situation a soldier's best friend is his weapon, because it is his one resource for disposing of the enemy, securing his own safety, and accomplishing the will of his captain.[11]

Then he quotes missionary Amy Carmichael:

> The only thing that matters is to throw all the energies of our being into the faithful use of this precious blade. Then, and only then, may we "rest our cause upon His Holy Word."[12]

For as long as we're on this earth, we will need to wear our armor and wield our sword. But as William Gurnall says so concisely: "Once [the Christian] enters the gates of that glorious city, he can say, 'Armour was for earth but robes are for heaven.'"[13]

# FOUR

# How Strong Can a Woman Be?

*The Lord gives the word [of power]; the women who bear and publish (the news) are a great host.* **Psalm 68:11,** *TAB*

TEN THOUSAND PEOPLE WERE ASKED RECENTLY, "Who has had the most positive influence on your religious faith?" "My mother," was the most frequent answer from every age group. "My wife," was the second-place response from men. The survey also showed women have a higher faith level than men.[1]

This poll simply proves what most of us knew all along: Women have a great deal of influence for God. This is both a privilege and a responsibility!

In the above verse the word *women* is sometimes rendered *company,* a military word. But this is not a conventional company of women soldiers. A loose translation of the verse would be, "The women who proclaim the news of victory are an army of praisers." Women may be considered less "muscular" than men, but our praising, praying, and proclaiming of the good news have the power to push back the forces that seek to destroy our loved ones and our communities!

Why is it that we are we so influential? Perhaps because women often feel things deeply. We are readily moved with compassion.

Quin's theory is that because women were created to give birth in the natural realm, we know more about travailing to give birth in the spiritual realm. We have a high tolerance for pain. We have the tenacity to stick it out until the birthing is done and our loved ones are brought from darkness into the light of Jesus.

A godly mother prays for her children from the time she first cradles her newborn in her arms. That prayer never stops. Like Jesus' mother, she ponders things in her heart (Lk 2:51). She talks often to God about that child she once nurtured in her womb.

"The hand that rocks the cradle is the hand that rules the world," wrote poet William Ross Wallace in the nineteenth century. We could paraphrase his thought: The one who "gives birth" in the spiritual realm is the one who prevails over the powers of darkness!

Sometimes on airplanes I'll ask my seatmate, "Is there anyone praying for you?" It's amazing how many times I'll get one of three answers: "My mother," "My grandmother," or "My wife."

## HURLING STONES AT THE ENEMY

We've all heard stories of a woman performing feats of superhuman strength—such as lifting the back of a car—when her child was in danger. The maternal instinct sends a surge of adrenaline through a woman, empowering her to do something thought impossible even for a well-muscled man. How much greater is the power the Holy Spirit gives to enable us in spiritual warfare.

Edith, a petite, graying mother, was puttering around her kitchen around 9:30 one Friday morning when a cold chill swept over her. Fear gripped her heart. "Dale is in danger," a voice said inside her. She immediately began praying for her engineer son. Five... ten... fifteen minutes she prayed. Then the burden lifted, and she went back to washing dishes.

That evening Dale called to tell her about his day. Around 9:30 that morning he had gone to inspect some remodeling work in the manufacturing plant where he worked. Suddenly he felt he should move out of the way. As he stepped aside, a huge steel beam fell to the floor, striking the very spot where he'd been standing seconds before.

In the natural realm Dale's little mom never could have deflected the fall of that steel beam. But because Edith was sensitive to the voice of the Holy Spirit as she worked in her kitchen that morning, her son's life was spared.

I like the account in the Old Testament about the Israelite woman who, when she saw King Abimelech approaching her city to burn it, took immediate and decisive action. Watching him from the top of the Tower of Thebez, she picked up a piece of a millstone and hurled it down on the wicked king's head. Too proud to have it said that a woman killed him, the king ordered his armorbearer to draw his sword and finish him off (see Jgs 9:50-57; 2 Sam 11:21).

Never let it be said that women are weak! They are still hurling stones at the enemy's plans. This unnamed woman of Thebez is one of a large company of women who continue to wreak havoc with Satan's plans.

## RUTHANNE MEETS THE ENEMY'S FLOOD

I learned in the midst of a crisis several years ago how strong a woman can be, though I didn't feel strong at the time. For months I had been eagerly learning about spiritual warfare, about Christ's authority over the devil, and about his investing us with that authority. But I really hadn't put it to the test.

One October unusually heavy rains had hit our Dallas area, and local radio stations warned of flash floods. That afternoon when it was time for me to pick up the neighborhood children from school, my husband John volunteered to go instead because of the bad weather.

Just after he left, the rain began to fall even harder, thundering like Niagara. Frightened, I looked out the front door and saw that water had filled the street and was now pouring down our sloping yard toward the house. Muddy water flooded the sidewalk and was quickly rising to porch level.

In a panic, I tried to brace a board across the porch entrance, then laid some old towels over the threshold of the front door. In seconds the rising water swept the board away and crept onto the small porch.

Suddenly I felt a righteous anger in my spirit and recognized I needed to take authority over the enemy's attempt to damage or destroy our home. No time to call my prayer partner or look up a Scripture verse. I just had to "wing it" on my own.

"Devil, in the name of Jesus, I forbid you to enter this house with muddy flood water," I shouted into the storm as I stood at the open front door. "This house belongs to God. It has been dedicated to him, and you have no right to enter and destroy it. In Jesus' name, I command this water to recede."

When I stopped shouting I realized the thundering noise had diminished and the rain was slackening. The water had come up to the threshold and the towels were wet. But as I watched, the flood water receded from the porch, formed a whirlpool below the step, then ran down the sidewalk and around the corner of the house.

For a moment I stood rooted to the spot, almost in shock that my desperate tactic had worked. Then I began to praise God for his faithfulness, acknowledging that he had given the victory. My husband was amazed when he got home and saw the mud silt on the porch that confirmed my story.

The following year we had another season of heavy rain, and flash flood warnings were again broadcast. I began taking authority over the devil as soon as I heard the news. I declared our home off-limits to Satan's destructive work. Though more rain fell that week than we'd had the previous October, flood waters never threatened our house. I learned the effectiveness of engaging in spiritual warfare before a situation reaches crisis proportions.

Of course, we have no power on our own; we must rely on the Holy Spirit's power. But operating in faith, not fear, is one way we can overcome the harassments of the devil.

I might add that I don't believe we are to indiscriminately "take authority" over bad weather. (In fact, in this case I didn't command the rain to cease.) But this kind of action is appropriate in certain situations when we're led by the Holy Spirit.

## CAN GOD USE ME?

What can one woman do? We've already looked at Deborah and the difference she made in the nation of Israel. Scripture gives many accounts of women who wielded godly influence in significant ways: Jochebed, Miriam, Hannah, Huldah, Esther, Ruth, Elizabeth, Mary, Dorcas, Priscilla, Phoebe, Joanna, and others.

Sometimes we need prayer plus action! Helen is an Alabama farmer's wife whose commitment to prayer has literally changed people's lives. Bonnie was one of her prayer projects.

Bonnie seemed to have everything required for happiness: a hard-working husband, two lovely children, a home, and many church friends. But peace and joy eluded her. Bonnie had been molested by her father, and she had allowed the seeds of hatred to grow in her heart to include all men. Turning to other women for love and acceptance, she'd gotten involved in lesbianism.

Bonnie became a Christian and got married, but still struggled with affections for her former lovers. She even preferred to dress like a male. Her ambivalent feelings made her so miserable that she came to Helen for help.

Bonnie would not admit that lesbianism is a sin—no matter how many Scriptures Helen showed her to the contrary. One day after Helen and her prayer partner had spent five hours praying with Bonnie to no avail, Helen told her, "I'm going to pray a prayer as though I'm you, and I want you to repeat it after me.

"Dear heavenly Father, I see in your Word that homosexuality is a sin. Therefore, lesbianism is a sin. Please forgive me for committing this sin."

"I can't say that because I don't think it is so," Bonnie argued, shaking her head.

Finally, after they prayed persistently, Bonnie got the words out of her mouth: "It is a sin, it is a sin. God, please forgive me." She began to sob—for the first time in many years—as the healing power of Jesus' forgiveness engulfed her.

Soon afterwards Helen took Bonnie to a women's conference. There she experienced godly love and affection from women. It was the beginning of a new life for her.

Helen determined to remain a strong force of love in Bonnie's life, showing her that she could have a healthy relationship with a woman friend. Whenever Bonnie asked for help, Helen responded. She helped her redecorate her home, then they worked on Bonnie's appearance—hairstyle, makeup, and clothes. Helen and her husband helped Bonnie plant a garden and later can some of the vegetables she grew.

When Bonnie's husband returned from a tour of duty overseas, he hardly recognized his wife, but he rejoiced at the changes. Some years later Bonnie went back to graduate school. Today she helps other people through her counseling ministry. Helen's willingness to stick it out now has reverberating effects in those to whom Bonnie ministers. This is a powerful example of what one woman with Jesus can do.

## A WRONG USE OF STRENGTH

God honors those who rely on his strength, but it is important that we women guard against manipulating people and circumstances to get what we want. Jezebel and her equally evil daughter Athaliah are two negative examples in the Bible.

When Ahab, king of northern Israel, married Jezebel, the daughter of a priest of Baal, he allowed her to bring idol worship to Israel. She was an idolator, a scheming murderer, and a controlling, domineering wife. The record says, "For there was no one who sold himself to do evil in the sight of the Lord as did Ahab, incited by his wife Jezebel" (1 Kgs 21:25, *TAB*). We read of her shameful end in 2 Kings chapter 9.

Athaliah followed her mother's evil example. She murdered her own grandsons in order to take the throne and rule over Judah, but in the end she also met a violent death (see 2 Kgs 11).

We women must avoid trying to manipulate circumstances (or God) in ways that are not God-directed. As we write this chapter, the local newspapers carry a story of a scheming woman's plans for revenge. A church pianist in a small Texas town, incensed that her thirteen-year-old daughter was edged out in cheerleader tryouts, was arrested for trying to arrange the murder of the rival teenager's mother.

One definition Webster gives of *manipulate* is, "to control or play upon by... insidious means, especially to one's own advantage." This method has no place in Spirit-led prayer and warfare.

We dare not attempt to manipulate God either. Rather, we

ask the Holy Spirit *how* to pray, for prayer comes from an intimate relationship with our Lord. We can count on miracles, rescues, healings, and supernatural events. But we cannot order them at will. We are working with a Commander who sees the "whole picture" while we see only a part. We need to trust him, each of us in our own trench, believing that he will lead us and those we love to victory.

## ENLARGING OUR BORDERS

Perhaps you feel your circle of influence is pretty small—consisting of your husband, your children, their school, your extended family, your church, your friends. If you are single your sphere may consist primarily of your work relationships, your family, your friends, and your church. If you're an "empty nester," you may feel your world is shrinking.

Have you ever considered that God might want to expand your horizon; to use you not only to pray for your family and friends, but for your city, state, or nation? Or another nation of the world?

Quin remembers how God began stretching her horizons and enlarging her borders:

My husband's job had just taken us to a different town, which I really didn't like very well. I complained to the Lord about it one day. Later, in my morning Bible reading, I stumbled across Jeremiah's message to God's people living in exile. It jumped from the page into my heart: "Build houses and settle down;... seek the peace and prosperity of the city to which I have carried you into exile. Pray to the LORD for it, because if it prospers, you too will prosper" (Jer 29:5a, 7).

Pray for the city where God had brought me? How could I? Where would I start? Because I knew nothing about spiritual warfare in those days, I just began praying about things I read in the daily newspaper. Not a bad place to start, really.

Years passed, and we moved to another area. In my Bible reading one day, verses from Isaiah sprang to life and challenged me to begin praying very specifically for the city where I now lived: "I have set watchmen upon your walls, O Jerusalem, who will never hold their peace day or night; you who [are His servants and by your prayers] put the Lord in remembrance [of His promises], keep not silence, and give Him no rest until He establishes Jerusalem and makes it a praise in the earth" (Is 62:6, 7, *TAB*).

In the place of *Jerusalem* I put the name of my city. And I wrote in my Bible: "God wants to station me as an intercessor sentry—a watchguard in prayer for my family and city. I'll need God's strategy to ambush the enemy's plan."

## TAKING STOCK OF THE CITY

I did some research on our sprawling resort area, asking such questions as: What is its historic background? Who first brought the gospel here? How many churches are there? How many bars? How can I identify with the needs of this community?

One day after fasting and prayer, a friend and I took a "prayer walk" in a two-block area of downtown. We passed an antique store with statues of Buddha in the window, a liquor store with a sign, "In Booze We Trust," a New Age store with a window display of crystals and weird head sculptures, a secret lodge temple, an Indian museum and burial mound, and an amusement palace with huge carved Tiki gods.

My heart was broken to see in only a two-block area so many things that surely displeased God. Yet I realized that not too many years ago, when I was in the enemy's camp, I would have thought all this was fine.

As we walked we bound the enemy's works of darkness and deception and asked the Holy Spirit to bring a revelation of Jesus Christ to the hearts of the people. Later we walked up and down and prayed on nearby streets, where psychics, go-go dancers, nightclubs, and liquor stores catered to summer tourists.

In time we enlisted other women who shared our vision to see righteousness become the standard for the city. Walking in pairs, we covered malls, schools, government buildings, residential neighborhoods, beaches, and parks.

Over the next few months a fortune-teller went out of business, one psychic shop shut down, and a teen nightclub closed its doors. We heard of other results later on, and we won't know the full affect of our spiritual warfare until we get to heaven. Though I have since moved, my prayer partners continue to assault the kingdom of darkness there, and more women are catching the vision of how they can make a difference through prayer.

John Dawson, author of *Taking Our Cities for God,* writes:

The fact is, there is a battle raging over your city and it is affecting you right now. Our individual blind spots and vices are usually common to the culture around us, and that culture is influenced by what the Bible calls principalities and powers (Eph 6:12, *KJV*).... Spiritual warfare begins at a personal level and escalates through layers of increasing difficulty—from personal and family to the realm of church life, and beyond that to the collective church in the city and the national and international realms.

Have you ever thought about the battle for your immediate neighborhood?... Several years ago my staff and I went on a prayer walk around our neighborhood. We stood in front of every house, rebuked Satan's work in Jesus' name, and prayed for a revelation of Jesus in the life of each family. We are still praying.... Today there are at least nine Christian families in the block where I live, and there is a definite sense of the Lord's peace.[2]

## CORPORATE PRAYER

Recently Quin had an opportunity to join more than four thousand Christian women for a two-hour prayer gathering on the steps of the United States Capitol building.

First we prayed for our nation. We asked God to give wisdom, knowledge, and understanding to all our government leaders. We engaged in corporate warfare against principalities and powers of darkness that have allowed abortion on demand, racism, humanism in our schools, widespread drug abuse, and an increase in crime, pornography, child abuse, and missing children.

Then we prayed for the women of America—the married, the divorced, the widowed, the single. We prayed for working mothers, for abused wives, for the wives and women of the military. We asked God to minister to their deepest needs and reveal himself to them.

We did not demonstrate or hold up signs; we just prayed. Afterwards small groups of women walked around the grounds of the capitol, praying for those who work there, then around the White House, the Supreme Court, and the various embassies. They prayed quietly for God's purposes to be accomplished in our nation.

Such a prayer effort by a few thousand women may appear to some to be purely symbolic. But I believe there is a spiritual dynamic in the prayers of agreement offered by those women that will make a difference in our nation.

## REPENTING FOR OUR NATION'S SINS

Soon after LeRoy and I moved to Dallas, we joined two thousand Christians gathered in front of City Hall to mark the eighteenth anniversary of the *Roe* v. *Wade* decision, which legalized abortion in America. We prayed silently, then corporately repented for the sins of our nation. A bell tolled twenty-seven times to represent the twenty-seven million babies killed since that infamous decision. Then we marched the six blocks to the Federal Courthouse, where that court case began, and continued our prayers.

It is meaningful to walk the ground where the devil is operating as we assault him. It is an outward declaration of God's victory in that place. As Joshua was about to march into the Promised Land, God told him: "I will give you every place where you set your foot, as I promised Moses.... Be strong and courageous, because you will lead these people to inherit the land.... Do not be terrified; do not be discouraged, for the LORD your God will be with you wherever you go" (Jos 1:3, 6, 9).

We can act upon this word today as the Holy Spirit shows us where to set our foot. But we must keep an attitude of humility and repentance as we pursue such a prayer project. John Dawson reminds us:

> As you stand in the gap for your city, allow the Holy Spirit to shine the bright light of truth into the inner rooms of your soul. Run from the religious deceit that would seduce you into believing that you are superior to any person. It is only by the blood of the Lamb and the power of the Spirit that we stand free from the chains of guilt and the sentence of death.[3]

## THE BATTLE IN THE HEAVENLIES

A big obstacle for many women in maintaining a consistent prayer life is the nagging question, "How can *my* prayers possibly make a difference in the way things turn out?" It is one of Satan's biggest ploys to dissuade us from pursuing prayer.

Yet Scripture clearly shows us that when believers pray on earth, they instigate activity in the heavenlies. The prophet Daniel had an angelic visitation after three weeks of praying, fasting, and repenting on behalf of his people. The angel told Daniel that on the first day he humbled himself to pray, God had heard his words. In fact, the angel had been dispatched with a message in response to Daniel's prayer, but he had encountered interference from the "prince of Persia." The messenger angel had to have help from the angel Michael to get through. He delivered a prophetic message to Daniel, and he indicated that on his return he would fight both the prince of Persia and the prince of Greece (see Dn 10:20).

If there were rulers in the spiritual realm (called princes) trying to stop Daniel's prayers from being answered, are we immune? No! I believe hostile spiritual forces still try to block our prayers from being answered. And Scripture implies that these evil princes rule over different geographical areas.

I assume our city has an evil prince over it, with other evil spirits working under him. While on my prayer walk, I bind any spirits I feel the Holy Spirit reveals to me: greed, adultery, idolatry, spiritual blindness, witchcraft, blasphemy, humanism, addiction, hatred, lying, murder, suicide, or whatever. I ask God to open blinded eyes so that people might turn from darkness to light and receive forgiveness through Jesus.

## THE COMFORTER HAS COME

The gift of the Holy Spirit empowers us to be strong women of God, even in our moments of weakness. Jesus promised his followers; "I will ask the Father, and He will give you another Comforter (Counselor, Helper, Intercessor, Advocate, Strengthener, and Standby) that He may remain with you forever; the Spirit of Truth.... He will teach you all things" (Jn 14:16, 17, 26, *TAB*).

Without this gift of the Holy Spirit, we would be power-less before the enemy. But he strengthens us for battle in many ways. Here are a few of them:

- The Holy Spirit testifies of Jesus (Jn 15:26; Rom 8:16).
- The Holy Spirit teaches (Lk 12:12; 1 Cor 2:13).
- The Holy Spirit guides (Mt 10:19, 20; Jn 16:13).
- The Holy Spirit reveals (Jn 14:20; 1 Cor 2:9, 10).
- The Holy Spirit comforts (Jn 14:16, 17; Acts 9:31).
- The Holy Spirit gives joy (Jn 15:11; Rom 14:17).
- The Holy Spirit gives spiritual gifts (1 Cor 12:4-31).
- The Holy Spirit liberates (Jn 8:32; Rom 8:2).
- The Holy Spirit empowers for service (Lk 4:14; Acts 1:8).
- The Holy Spirit intercedes for us (Rom 8:26; 1 Cor 14:14, 15).

When we ask the Holy Spirit to intercede through us, many Christians believe this means to seek God's will and then pray accordingly. Still others believe it involves praying in an unknown tongue as those in the early Christian church. Because of this, in a book on spiritual warfare it seems fair to include this particular "weapon."

Consider Paul's words: "... the Spirit helps us in our weaknesses. We do not know what we ought to pray, but the Spirit himself intercedes for us with groans that words can-not express. And he who searches our hearts knows the mind of the Spirit, because the Spirit intercedes for the saints in accordance with God's will" (Rom 8:26b, 27).

"For anyone who speaks in a tongue does not speak to men but to God" (1 Cor 14:2).

"I will pray with the spirit, and I will pray with the understanding also..." (1 Cor 14:15a, *KJV*).

Interceding according to the will of God is the most important ingredient of prayer.

Judson Cornwall, author of numerous Christian books, explains the use of tongues in prayer:

> Prayer is the most valuable use of tongues for it is "speaking to God" (1 Cor 14:2).
>
> ... The Holy Spirit is certainly not limited to the English language, nor is He confined to modern languages. He has access to every language ever used by mankind, and He is very familiar with the language used in heaven. When deep intercession is needed, the Spirit often uses a language that is beyond the intellectual grasp of the speaker to bypass the censorship of his or her conscious mind, thereby enabling the Spirit to say what needs to be prayed without arguing with the faith level of the one through whom the intercession flows.
>
> Praying in tongues is not the work of the subconscious. It's really *supra-intellectual* praying. That is, the prayer is beyond the natural mind, not beneath the conscious level. Intercessory prayer in tongues is not incoherent speech. The very words are motivated by the Holy Spirit, addressed to the Father and approved by the Lord Jesus (see Mk 16:17).[4]

According to Acts 2:39 the gift is available to all bornagain Christians—not just those who lived in the first century after Christ. The only requirements are that you be God's child, and that you ask (see Lk 11:11-13).

In the years since my (Quin's) prayer life has taken on new meaning, I have kept a prayer journal of my prayers and God's answers. (I tell about it in *How to Pray for Your Children* and *How to Pray for Your Family and Friends*.) But my prayer time is not limited to the time I sit in my gold den chair for morning devotions. I pray while ironing, working in the kitchen, driving, walking, writing, speaking, cleaning house, lying in bed—trying always to keep my ears tuned to the voice of the Holy Spirit.

## PRAYING WITH A PARTNER

Sometimes we pray and do warfare effectively for someone else's need, but our faith seems weak when it comes to fighting our own personal battles. That's when it's good to have a prayer partner to encourage us and to pray prayers of agreement (see Dt 32:30).

Cathy was a single working woman facing a seemingly impossible financial problem. She had to have emergency gallbladder surgery, and her insurance company would not cover the medical bills. One night Cathy and her prayer partner Quinett (Quin's daughter) began to pray about the enormous debt.

"We came against the powers of darkness, demanding them to loose money for Cathy's medical bill," Quinett said. "We had no idea where the money might come from, but we continued our warfare for about thirty minutes. Finally we felt total peace about it, so we went to the kitchen and cooked supper."

As the weeks passed and the bills kept coming from the

doctors and the hospital, Cathy skipped meals so she could send small regular payments. Then began the phone calls saying her accounts would be turned over to a collection agency if she didn't pay. But she still maintained the God-given peace she'd felt when she and Quinett had prayed months earlier.

One day Cathy got a letter from the insurance company saying they definitely would not cover any of the costs. Cathy turned to a coworker and said, "It doesn't look like my insurance will come through, but Jesus will."

The colleague rolled her eyes as if to say, "Yeah, Cathy. Like how?"

Eight months later, without any explanation, the insurance company sent a check to cover eighty percent of the costs. By this time Cathy had paid the rest. What caused an insurance company to reverse its decision? Cathy and Quinett can only say they did what the Holy Spirit led them to do, and God took care of the rest.

## STRATEGY FOR WARFARE

By now you've gotten the picture that every battle differs. So does the strategy. One woman told us, "I believe the Lord desires us to have a militant attitude, serving as watchmen for those he calls us to stand in the prayer gap for. No sleeping, no deciding to change your mind, no laziness—just consistently and diligently bombarding the enemy and praising God for his answers that are on the way. The Lord loves a tenacious warrior who is ready to take a spiritual warfare assignment at a moment's notice."

Another friend suggests three principles to help us keep our warfare in proper perspective:

**A**ggressive toward the enemy;
**R**uthless with our own fleshly pride and selfishness;
**T**olerant and loving toward one another.

Thus we have an acrostic, the ART of spiritual warfare.

How strong can a woman be? As strong as she will allow the Holy Spirit to be through her. But becoming that vessel the Holy Spirit can use requires discipline. And that's the topic of our next chapter.

# FIVE

# The Disciplines of the Spirit-Empowered Woman

*"For if you remain silent at this time, relief and deliverance for the Jews will arise from another place, but you and your father's family will perish. And who knows but that you have come to royal position for such a time as this?" Then Esther sent this reply to Mordecai: "... I and my maids will fast as you do. When this is done, I will go to the king,... And if I perish, I perish."* **Esther 4:14-16**

Q UEEN ESTHER is a biblical example of how strong a woman can be. When facing a crisis that threatened the annihilation of the Jews, she called for a period of fasting and prayer before she took action on her own. Then she put her life on the line by going to the king and intervening for her people's lives.

Perhaps the greatest lessons we can learn from Esther are *discipline* and *balance*. She did not rush to implement a plan of her own without seeking God's direction. Nor did she take a passive role and say, "If God wants to do something, he can do it." Disciplining herself and her people through a fast, she balanced that by taking action one step at a time.

## DISCIPLINE AND DESTINY

Esther's story provides an excellent model for fighting our own tough spiritual battles. Long before she was selected as one of the candidates to be queen, Esther learned the discipline of obedience. She willingly obeyed instructions from Mordecai, her foster father. Then she submitted to a disciplined year of preparation before she was presented to the king. Even after being crowned queen of Persia, she continued to follow Mordecai's godly counsel.

Mordecai told her of the nobleman Haman's edict calling for all the Jews to be killed on a certain day. Mordecai asked her to go before the king and plead for mercy. As the story unfolds we see Esther following three important principles:

1. She settled in her heart that this battle was one in which she should be involved. She was in the palace "for such a time as this," and her commitment was solid.
2. She called the Jewish people to a fast, recognizing a solution was beyond her human wisdom. She would have to rely totally upon God.
3. She took action one step at a time, expecting God's direction at each juncture.

God granted Esther favor, and the king held out his

scepter to receive her. But instead of presenting her petition just then, she invited him and Haman to a banquet she had prepared. At the table that evening she still didn't reveal her request, though the king gave her the opportunity. She was obviously aware of the importance of timing. She simply asked the two men to come to another banquet the following day.

God intervened again by giving the king a sleepless night. The ensuing events caused the tables to be turned on wicked Haman, and he was hung on the gallows he had built for Mordecai. This was a victory far greater than Esther could have imagined. God intervened to "reverse the curse" against the Jews, and they were spared.

In the end, Haman's entire estate was given to Esther, and Mordecai was promoted to second in command under the king.

## TRAINING THAT MOLDS

"What is the most important thing you've learned through your experiences in spiritual warfare?" we asked a number of seasoned intercessors.

Many responded, "Discipline"—that quality so essential to victory but so distasteful to the flesh. Who doesn't want to win in a skirmish with the enemy? Yet few of us easily submit to the discipline and dying to self necessary to overcome Satan's onslaughts.

"The enemy can use our own ignorance against us," one intercessor responded. "He knows the law that will bring accusations to those who are trying to live up to its standard.

We must discipline ourselves to learn God's Word and use it as a weapon against the attacks of the enemy."

"Probably the most significant lesson I learned was the importance of disciplining my tongue—no gossip, backbiting, silly talk, coarse jesting," another wrote. "In prayer and warfare we should use our tongues according to the Word of God. It's also important to be led by the Holy Spirit in what we say to other people."

"I must always be prepared, try never to let my guard down," a third person said, "and listen continually for the voice of the Holy Spirit."

Webster defines *discipline* as "training that corrects, molds, or perfects the mental faculties or moral character." Our yielding to the correcting, molding, and perfecting work of the Holy Spirit can be painful, but it pays rich dividends by making us effective spiritual warriors.


WHY FAST ANYWAY?

Esther's immediate response to crisis was to call for a fast in preparation for her intercession before the king. It seems quite plausible that during the fast God revealed to Esther the strategy she was to follow. In like manner, fasting can become a weapon of warfare for us to receive God's guidance.

The prophetess Anna is an example of an intercessor who, like Esther, was in the right place at the right time. For years she had been in the temple ministering to the Lord with fasting and prayers. The Spirit led Anna to enter a certain area of the temple at the exact moment Mary and Joseph arrived with the infant Jesus. Recognizing that he was indeed the promised Messiah, she broadcast the good news. Her years of prayer and fasting were richly rewarded.

*Dake's Annotated Reference Bible* offers the view that fasting is the antidote for unbelief:

The disciples asked the Lord why they could not heal a lunatic boy. Jesus said, "Because of your unbelief.... Howbeit this kind goeth not out but by prayer and fasting" (Mt 17:20, 21, *KJV*). Faith needs prayer for its development and full growth, and prayer needs fasting for the same reason.... To fast means to abstain from food—that which caused the fall of man.

Fasting humbles the soul before God, chastens the soul, and crucifies the appetites and denies them so as to give time to prayer. It manifests earnestness before God to the exclusion of all else, shows obedience, gives the digestive system a rest, demonstrates the mastery of man over appetites, aids in temptation, helps to attain power over demons, develops faith, crucifies unbelief, and aids in prayer.[1]

Some Christians are reluctant to fast because they fear it can lead to fanaticism or occultism. We are aware that fasting is practiced by spiritists and adherents of false religions to sharpen their sensitivities to the spiritual realm and even to invite demons to give them power. But Jesus spoke of fasting at the same time he taught his followers how to pray and how to give. All three are disciplines the Christian should observe (see Mt 6:1-18).

In his excellent book *God's Chosen Fast*, Arthur Wallis writes:

We must not think of fasting as a hunger strike designed to force God's hand and get our own way! Prayer, however, is more complex than simply asking a loving father to supply his child's needs. Prayer is warfare. Prayer is wrestling. There are opposing forces. There are spiritual cross currents.

... The man who prays with fasting is giving heaven notice that he is truly in earnest; that he will not give up nor let God go without the blessing.

... You should expect that a season of fasting would prove to be for you, as it was for your Master, a time of conflict with the powers of darkness. Satan will often try to take advantage of your physical condition to launch an attack. Discouragement is one of his weapons. Guard against it by maintaining a spirit of praise.[2]

We see that setting captives free is also a scriptural purpose for fasting. God asks, "Is not this the kind of fasting I have chosen: to loose the chains of injustice and untie the cords of the yoke, to set the oppressed free and break every yoke?" (Is 58:6).

## PUSHING BACK THE ENEMY

Erby, a "modern-day Anna," experienced the power of fasting and prayer in the lives of Pastor Sam Phillips and his wife, Gloria, who suffered from a crippling disease and subsequent discouragement.

Soon after Erby started working for the Phillips family as a housekeeper, she began praying daily that they would receive the enabling power of the Holy Spirit in their lives. The Lord expressly warned Erby not to open her mouth to Sam and Gloria about spiritual matters. Also, she was not to open her mouth to eat anything on the days she worked for them. She was to pray—period.

Many days Erby fussed with God for making her fast and keep quiet about spiritual things, when she saw so many opportunities to speak. But he would not grant her that liberty. For four years Erby never opened her mouth to Sam and Gloria; but oh, how she talked to God! Meanwhile, Gloria seemed to be getting worse.

Erby would clean all the household furniture, praying as she went, claiming that its owners would make a deeper commitment to Jesus. She prayed over their bathtub, their drapes, their doorknobs, their refrigerator, their sink. To Erby, the whole Phillips house became an altar of prayer. She sanctified every inch of it, and kept commanding the devil to move back and take his hands off God's property.

The day came when Gloria spoke sharply to Erby, then hobbled off to her bedroom to end her misery with a handful of pills. The Lord showed Erby what was about to happen, but still he made her keep quiet. She cried out, "Oh God! By your Holy Spirit, I know what's about to happen in that room! I can't go in there, but you can, Lord. And I ask you to go in, in the power of the name of Jesus, and stop what is about to take place."

God heard Erby's supplications. Gloria Phillips did not swallow the fistful of pills in her hand. Later she and Pastor Sam were renewed in their faith. God finally allowed Erby to speak and instruct Gloria in the ways of God. Gloria was healed of her disease, and today she teaches Scripture. Her testimony in *A Heart Set Free* gives credit and thanks to Erby, her faithful household helper, who persevered for four difficult years—praying, fasting, warring against the devil, and believing God for her healing.[3]

Gloria told Quin how her three small daughters loved Erby and responded to the Spirit of God in her during those difficult days. The integrity of Erby's Christian walk spoke loud and clear, even when she was silent.

## TREASURES OF DARKNESS

While fasting is a discipline many Christians choose to ignore, there is another discipline that none of us can ignore: hardship and adversity. Paul wrote to Timothy: "You therefore must endure hardship as a good soldier of Jesus Christ. No one engaged in warfare entangles himself with the affairs of this life, that he may please him who enlisted him as a soldier" (2 Tm 2:3-4, *NKJV*).

During a difficult period in my own life several years ago, I developed the habit of walking a mile every day to talk to the Lord and settle my thoughts. I was dealing with a rebellious teenager, caring for my invalid in-laws living in our home, and trying to cope with financial pressures and myriad problems while my husband traveled frequently. I struggled against self-pity and the feeling that I was shouldering the load alone.

On my walk one crisp October morning the Lord spoke to me through Isaiah 45:3: "I will give you the treasures of darkness, riches stored in secret places, so that you may know that I am the LORD, the God of Israel, who summons you by name."

Then he said very clearly, "Ruthanne, these are precious days. I am teaching you the treasures of darkness."

I desperately wanted God to quickly solve all these problems; they certainly didn't seem "precious" to my natural mind. Yet I knew they weren't going to evaporate overnight. The Lord said he was teaching me as I allowed him to; there was value in the experience. I remembered reading of Jesus, "Although he was a son, he learned obedience from what he suffered" (Heb 5:8).

After that morning with the Lord under the trees, my circumstances actually got worse, not better. But I began to see that from God's point of view, my response to the difficulties was more important than the problems themselves. He obviously wanted to change me, and I finally consented.

I have come to believe that God does his best work in darkness: in creation, in the incarnation, in the Garden of Gethsemane, at Calvary, in my own "dark night of the soul."

The glory of it all for me was not just seeing circumstances change, which they eventually did. The greater blessing was allowing God to change me. And in the process I came to know God and his character in a way that only adversity can teach.

## THE BATTLE OF THE MIND

"We demolish arguments and every pretension that sets itself up against the knowledge of God, and we take captive every thought to make it obedient to Christ" (2 Cor 10:5).

All who enter the arena of spiritual warfare quickly learn that their mind is a battleground bombarded with doubt, discouragement, false accusations, and mockery from Satan and his emissaries. But we can ask the Holy Spirit to empower us to take captive our false thoughts and to make them obedient to Christ.

Ann had an effective ministry of counseling, deliverance, and teaching. Then circumstances required her to pull back from "public ministry" to care for her invalid parents. She knew this was God's plan for her, but it was a difficult adjustment. She shares her experience of learning to discipline her mind:

"As time passed, I began to have more and more negative thoughts about everything, but especially about myself. I believed every 'tear down' thought that wandered past. It seemed I couldn't trust myself to hear the Lord; every negative Scripture in the Word seemed aimed at me. Down and down I went. No longer any balance—just negative.

"I was finally fighting thoughts attacking my salvation. I couldn't pray, couldn't read the Word—and I didn't want to.

"Then one night the Lord told me to write a list of the good things about myself. I explained I had none, but he assured me he would show me this was untrue. And he began to give me the list.

"I argued every point in the beginning. For example, he said I had compassion. I could only feel the hardness of my heart. He went on to remind me of instances where I had shown compassion for Mom.

"As we went on I had a thought: Satan stands before the throne accusing believers (see Rv 12:10). So that gives new meaning to the Scripture that tells us to think on the good things (see Phil 4:8). The good report is needed to balance the thrusts of the wicked one, for oneself as well as for others.

"The Lord showed me that the mind is a battlefield. Enemy ammunition flies around. It is to be avoided. If you caress it and claim it, it's yours. It is wise to counterattack with your own ammunition—the list of good things God has spoken to you, in addition to the written Word. Knowing that the Lord has given this ammunition is so powerful for the tearing down of strongholds.

"When the enemy returns, I can say, 'Satan, the Lord says I do have compassion. I'll not receive the lies you are telling me.'

"This has released me. Now I feel more comfortable going to the Word, not because I have to (which leads to guilt) but because the desire is there. Now I can more quickly smile, and I walk with less of a burden."

## UNTO THE GLORY OF GOD

As we submit to these disciplines of prayer, fasting, patience in hardship, and controlling our thoughts, we truly can become women warriors empowered by the Holy Spirit. And all that we do will be to the glory of God our Father.

Lou struggled to discipline her tongue. Her elderly mother had moved from another city to the apartment behind Lou's house. In the difficult adjustment to a different church and new surroundings, she would often vent her frustrations on Lou.

"Well, everyone doesn't teach Sunday school for the right

reasons," she said testily one day when Lou was talking about plans for her next lesson.

"Mother, I get the message," Lou snapped, then walked out of the room.

A few days later she shared the experience with her prayer partner, Nita, as they worked on plans for a reception. "I know I should control my tongue," Lou groaned, "but Mom's criticism just sets me off."

"When you said what you did, you received her message as if it were true," Nita told her. "You need to cancel those words and speak the truth instead. Let's go for a prayer walk while you begin to declare, 'I do all things unto the glory of God.'"

As Lou made her declaration, she and Nita walked to the church fellowship hall to continue their planning. Upon entering the building, the first thing they saw was a dedication plaque with a large inscription: *Unto the glory of God.*

"There's your confirmation," Nita said. "You just need to remember to keep declaring it!"

Many twentieth-century Esthers and Annas have come to their "royal positions" for such a time as this. Discipline and balance—doing what we need to do to cooperate with God—are hallmarks of Spirit-empowered women.

# SIX

# Our Weapons and Strategy

*For though we live in the world, we do not wage war as the world does. The weapons we fight with are not the weapons of the world. On the contrary, they have divine power to demolish strongholds.* **2 Corinthians 10:3, 4**

*Put on God's whole armor... that you may be able successfully to stand up against [all] the strategies and the deceits of the devil.* **Ephesians 6:11, TAB**

"IN THE NAME OF JESUS, you give that purse back to me," Kay shouted as she chased a young teenager across the grocery store parking lot. "I earned that money, and you have no right to it."

As she grabbed the scared kid by the arm and jerked her purse out of his hand, he broke down crying. It was his first time to try snatching someone's purse as he'd seen his older buddies do. But he picked the wrong young woman in this case—or the right one, depending on how you look at it.

Kay knows she has authority in the name of Jesus, and she

instinctively responded to the challenge without thinking of the possible dangers. She began sharing the gospel with the youngster, explaining that he needed to accept Jesus as Savior, then trust God to provide him a job. He walked away visibly shaken.

"Kay, you could have gotten hurt!" Ruthanne said when she told her about the incident. Kay was a convert from the drug culture, now attending Bible school. The store where she had stopped was a known trouble spot for thievery.

"I had just gotten paid at work, and I needed that money to pay my school bill," she said. "No way was I going to let the devil steal from me!"

## THE NAME OF JESUS

We've already established that our conflict is with an invisible enemy and his evil agents in the spiritual realm, who operate through individuals. We cannot use physical weapons against enemy agents, but God has given us invisible spiritual weapons. Kay used one of the primary weapons, the name of Jesus. Consider these Scriptures:

"You are my King and my God,... Through you we push back our enemies; through your name we trample our foes. I do not trust in my bow, my sword does not bring me victory; but you give us victory over our enemies, you put our adversaries to shame" (Ps 44:4-7).

"The seventy-two returned with joy, and said, 'Lord, even the demons submit to us in your name.' He replied, ' ... I have given you authority to trample on snakes and scorpions and to overcome all the power of the enemy; nothing will harm you' " (Lk 10:17-19).

"They overcame him [Satan] by the blood of the Lamb and by the word of their testimony" (Rv 12:11).

The only way to use the name of Jesus as a weapon is to speak to the enemy. Jesus spoke to Satan in the wilderness (see Lk 4:4, 8, 12); he also spoke to a fig tree and cursed it (see Mt 21:19). So don't feel reticent about speaking to the evil powers of darkness. Paul Billheimer says:

> Many believers have been so tyrannized and dominated by Satan and the prevailing theology of Satan's power and invincibility that, like me, they would never dare to speak directly to him, even in the name of Jesus. For years, I couldn't imagine Satan running away. The picture that had frightened and terrified me was of Satan on the attack, "going about like a roaring lion, seeking whom he may devour" (1 Pt 5:8). James' exhortation to resist encouraged me to face that roaring lion [see Jas 4:7]. When I mustered enough courage to speak directly to him in the name of Jesus, it was a great surprise to me to discover an immediate sense of deliverance—as though he had vanished, melted away.
>
> … The only way we can be sure that he knows we are resisting him is to *speak aloud,* to directly and audibly confront him with the truth.
>
> May I remind you again that *our resistance* by itself is not what causes Satan to flee; he flees because of the *power of Jesus* which is ours through prayer.[1]

Bible teacher Dean Sherman expands on this thought:

> Man… has authority, based on what Christ did on the Cross and through His resurrection. Man can still employ

Satan through selfishness and sin, but the balance of power on the earth rests with man in the name of Jesus Christ. The authority is complete in man as long as man is in relationship with God through Jesus Christ. With our authority comes the responsibility to use it for God's purposes. If we don't rebuke the devil, he will not be rebuked. If we don't drive him back, he will not leave. It is up to us. Satan knows of our authority, but hopes we will stay ignorant. We must be as convinced of our authority as the devil is.[2]

## THE BLOOD OF JESUS

The sacrificial death, burial, and resurrection of Jesus is the basis of our victory over Satan. He is the sinless sacrifice, the "Lamb that was slain from the creation of the world" (Rv 13:8). In order to redeem us, Jesus had to come to earth in human form, as Hebrews declares: "Since the children have flesh and blood, he too shared in their humanity so that by his death he might destroy him who holds the power of death—that is, the devil—and free those who all their lives were held in slavery by their fear of death" (Heb 2:14, 15).

When we confess our sins and repent (meaning to *turn* from sin), the blood of Jesus cleanses us and puts us in right relationship with God. We call it being "born again." When we have this experience, we are not only protected by the blood of Jesus; we are authorized to use the blood as a weapon of warfare. H.A. Maxwell Whyte says:

The destroyer cannot get in under the Blood-line where it has been placed. But, unfortunately, too many have been loosely taught that "Satan cannot get through the Blood-line." They have not been informed that *Satan can and does get through if the Blood-line is let down.* And how do we let it down? *By disobedience.*

We can hardly claim to be under the Blood of Jesus if we are walking in deliberate disobedience.... Sprinkling of the Blood of Jesus without obedience to the Word of God will avail us nothing.[3]

To "plead the blood of Jesus" means to appropriate our Savior's shed blood as protection from the evil one. The practice is based on the Passover, when the blood of a lamb was applied to the doorpost and lintels of every Jewish home, protecting the inhabitants from the death angel who would pass through Egypt and take the oldest male of every family. The angel passed over those homes that were under the blood (see Ex 12:1-13).

Of course, the blood of lambs and other animals was a temporary solution for sin. Only the shedding and appropriating of Jesus' blood provided a permanent atonement. Whyte writes:

In the natural world, we would have no difficulty understanding how to apply disinfectant to an infection. We would take the disinfectant and sprinkle or pour it upon the infection, and the result would be that all germs and living organisms present in that infection would die.

Now we should have no difficulty in doing the same thing spiritually. Wherever Satan is at work, we must apply the only corrective antidote there is—the Blood of Jesus. There is absolutely no alternative, no substitute.

Prayer, praise, worship, and devotion all have their part in our approach to God; but the Blood of Jesus is the only effective counteragent to corruption.

This is why Satan has always tried to take the Blood out of our churches. If there is no disinfectant, then his demons are free to continue their deadly work of destruction in spirit, soul, and body.

... In every situation where you sense that you are under the attack of Satan or needing special protection, *that* is the time to plead the Blood. By so doing, you are reminding God that you are trusting in His mercy; you are reminding Satan that he cannot touch you as long as you are under the Blood; and you are reminding yourself of the ground of your confidence in Christ.[4]

## THE POWER OF THE BLOOD

Ruthanne learned in a dramatic way the power of the blood of Jesus to protect his children from Satan:

My husband, John, went on a mission outreach to Haiti with a group of his students. One Sunday afternoon he joined two other missionaries who were driving around a mountain not far from Port-au-Prince to visit a remote village church. Leaving the main road, they drove some distance on a small "goat track" road, then parked the jeep and walked the rest of the way.

On the return trip John drove. As he inched around the small road, he couldn't see over the nose of the jeep because of the incline. Suddenly he realized the right front wheel had gone off the road. The missionary in the front seat immediately began crying out, "The blood of Jesus! The blood of Jesus! The blood of Jesus!"

The jeep, by all the laws of physics, should have crashed down to the valley several hundred feet below. Instead it moved upward, spanned a gap between the road and a boulder, and stopped. The front differential rested on a rock on the other side of the gap. The left rear wheel was the only wheel on solid ground; the other three were spinning in space.

John and the missionaries climbed out of the jeep on the uphill side and had a thanksgiving service in the middle of the road. At that moment the pastor John had preached for that morning drove up in his small truck. "I was praying for you, and I had a feeling I needed to come and check on you," he said. A group of students were with him, and they helped maneuver the jeep onto the main road so they could get it down the mountain. The only damage was a warped driveshaft.

As they drove on, they came upon a group of men carrying a Haitian's body from a ravine below up to the roadside. He had been killed when his car crashed some minutes before John's near brush with death.

"I had the feeling that a malevolent spirit was determined to kill someone on that road," John said. "When his efforts to kill three missionaries were thwarted, it seems he took revenge on someone with no divine protection.

"After I returned to Dallas, an intercessor friend told me the Holy Spirit had given her and a group of students a burden to pray for my safety on that trip," John said. They had prayed fervently two weeks before I'd even left; the Holy Spirit showed my friend that the devil would try to kill me in Haiti. Later a missionary friend told me that the road has a voodoo curse on it, and a certain number of people are killed on it every year. Thank God for the power of prayer and the protection of the blood of Jesus!"

Arthur Mathews declares: "The only man [or woman] who can keep the enemy at bay is the intercessor, and blessed is that intercessor who knows how to use the power of the blood in spiritual warfare."[5]

## PRAISE AS A WEAPON

"Jehoshaphat appointed men to sing to the LORD and to praise him for the splendor of his holiness as they went out at the head of the army,... As they began to sing and praise, the LORD set ambushes against the men... who were invading Judah, and they were defeated" (2 Chr 20:21, 22).

Praise has a threefold purpose in spiritual warfare. First, it glorifies God and keeps our focus on him and his power. Second, it terrifies the enemy and throws his ranks into confusion. In the scriptural example just cited, Judah's three enemies became so confused they killed one another! Third, praise encourages the believer as he or she proclaims the victory in the spiritual realm before it is manifested in the natural realm.

Walking in a spirit of praise helps us remember that we fight from a position of victory, not defeat (Eph 1:18-23). Often when circumstances look totally bleak, we are on the threshold of a breakthrough. The enemy hurls his worst shot just before his defeat is sealed. Therefore, it is always too soon to quit!

The psalmist wrote, "He makes the [storm] clouds his chariot" (Ps 104:3). Arthur Mathews reminds us: "Nowhere is the greatness of God seen to such advantage as it is in His ability to use as His chariot of conquest the circumstances that pose the greatest threat to His cause."[6]

## STAND AGAINST SATAN'S STRATEGIES

Paul warned the early Christians to stand against the devil's "wiles" or strategies (Eph 6:11).

Strategy is the science and art of conducting a military campaign on a broad scale. You set the goal, then devise methods for achieving that goal. Tactics are the specific methods you employ to fulfill the strategy plan. A military commander devises a strategy for the overall campaign, then the tactics to fulfill it, based upon reports from intelligence agents and surveillance equipment.

If the devil has schemes, or military strategies, then we need God's strategy for the specific battles he calls us to fight. The Holy Spirit is the intelligence agent who knows the enemy's strategy and tactics; it is critical for us to seek his guidance and fight our battles accordingly.

## QUIN'S STRATEGY LESSONS

As a young Christian, Quin reports, I thought I could fight every giant, pray for every troubled marriage, intercede for any problem—whether people asked for prayer or not! It wasn't long before I was physically spent. I learned mainly by trial and error in those days that not every battle is mine, and not every battle strategy is the same. We cannot "standardize" spiritual warfare. I'm amazed at how many different battle plans are in the Bible.

David learned to inquire of the Lord, "Shall I go to battle?" Sometimes the Lord would say yes, or he might give different instructions. Once he told David to wait until he heard the sound of marching in the tops of the mulberry trees!

When I'm seeking God's guidance for spiritual battle, I use what I call a Four-W strategy: Worship—Wait—Word—Warfare. I *worship* the Lord, then *wait* in his presence until he quickens something in his *Word* to use in *warfare* against the enemy in the battle at hand.

Once a boy was giving my teenage son some foolish advice. I prayed as David did when his son Absalom was getting wrong counsel. "Lord, let the advice he's getting be as foolishness" (see 2 Sm 15:31). Not long afterwards, my son admitted it was "foolish stuff" his friend was telling him.

But the next time one of his peers was adversely affecting my son, God reminded me that Job's bondage was broken when he prayed for his friends. My husband and I began to pray two things for my son's friend: God's blessings to shower him and for God's will to be done in his life. Amazingly, he received an athletic scholarship from an out-of-town school and was removed from our son's life within a few weeks. God blessed him by providing his college tuition, and he also came to know Jesus as Lord!

We, just can't improve on God's strategy. His best often surpasses what we can ask or even think.

## THE BATTLE CRY

Quin admits that her "quiet time" isn't always quiet: I like to pray aloud, shout, stamp my feet, laugh, and clap. At other times I may be very quiet, praying silently with hands uplifted, bowing or lying prostrated on the floor.

Many Scripture passages encourage some volume in our prayer: "Clap your hands, all you nations; shout to God with cries of joy" (Ps 47:1).

"Sing, O Daughter of Zion; shout aloud, O Israel! Be glad and rejoice with all your heart, O Daughter of Jerusalem! The Lord has... turned back your enemy" (Zep 3:14, 15a).

I sometimes shout *before* I've seen any signs of victory in the natural, just as the Israelites did before the walls of Jericho collapsed. God's battle plan called for them to march for six days in silence, then shout aloud at the sound of the trumpet.

Sometimes we need to raise a battle cry, a shout, as part of our spiritual warfare strategy. Shouting was definitely part of my war-room tactic when I lived in the country with no close neighbors. Since a recent move into a city apartment, I try to be less noisy.

Our mouths are our most effective means of using our spiritual weapons. God says his Word will not return void (Is 55:11), so I use my tongue to praise him and to war against demonic power.

## HE TRAINS MY HANDS FOR WAR

I also use my hands in warfare intercession. David said, "Praise be to the LORD, my Rock, who trains my hands for war, my fingers for battle" (Ps 144:1).

I once did a word study on the hand, and I was thrilled to discover many Scriptures related to God's hand and warfare:

"Your right hand, O LORD, was majestic in power. Your right hand, O LORD, shattered the enemy" (Ex 15:6).

"My soul clings to you; your right hand upholds me" (Ps 63:8).

"For he [God] stands at the right hand of the needy one" (Ps 109:31).

"For I am the LORD, your God, who takes hold of your right hand and says to you, Do not fear; I will help you" (Is 41:13).

In studying the Hebrew word for *hand,* I found that one form of the word means "open hand," while another form means "closed hand." In prayer I extend my open hand to the Lord, beseeching him on behalf of the person I'm interceding for. In warfare I close my other hand into a fist and shake it at Satan, as I declare the Word of God on behalf of the one for whom I'm battling: "Satan, it is written, the Son of Man—Jesus Christ—came to save the lost. It is not his will that any perish, so take your hands off my brother. He shall declare the praises of the most high God."

I also clap my hands—loudly, even in my city apartment. I see two reasons for this in the Bible: to praise the Lord and to mock God's enemy (see Ps 47:1; Lam 2:15).

"This is what the Sovereign LORD says: Strike your hands together and stamp your feet and cry out 'Alas!' because of all the wicked and detestable practices of the house of Israel" (Ez 6:11).

"So then, son of man, prophesy and strike your hands together. Let the sword strike twice, even three times" (Ez 21:14a).

Striking my hands together, I may say, "You spirit of discouragement, be gone today. You have no place in this home, which is dedicated to the Lord God of hosts."

Still clapping, I applaud the Lord.

"Thank you, Lord, for your spirit of peace. For your joy I applaud you, for you are on the throne today. You are king of my life and my home. I acknowledge that nothing is impossible with you, Lord."

Our bodies can be used in worship and in warfare. My mother used to raise both her hands before the Lord because God told us to lift up holy hands to him, without doubting (see 1 Tm 2:8). Wiggling her fingers, she'd declare, "Lord, these represent my ten grandchildren," and she'd name them. "I'm standing in the prayer gap for them. Lord, may they love and serve you all their lives. Give wisdom and understanding, knowledge and strength this day, in Jesus' name." Then she'd pray for their individual needs—a school test, a boyfriend problem, or a health concern.

God gave us a body and creative ways to praise him with it—as well as to use in warfare against his enemy. So our prayer times need not be dull!

## THE WEAPON OF JOY

"The righteous will see and fear; they will laugh at him, saying, 'Here now is the man who did not make God his stronghold'" (Ps 52:6, 7b).

"The Virgin Daughter of Zion despises you and mocks you [Sennacherib, king of Assyria].... Who is it you have insulted and blasphemed?" (2 Kgs 19:21-22).

*Laugh* in the biblical sense includes the meanings "to mock, to play, to make sport, to deride, to laugh to scorn."

There is also a laugh that is merry, and it does our hearts good like a medicine (Prv 17:22).

David wrote: "When the Lord brought back the captives to Zion... our mouths were filled with laughter, our tongues with songs of joy" (Ps 126:1a, 2).

Examples of women in the Bible who rejoiced are Miriam (Ex 15:20-21), Hannah (1 Sm 2:1-10), and Mary (Lk 1:46-55).

Paul wrote: "Rejoice in the Lord always. I will say it again: Rejoice!" (Phil 4:4).

Anne, a young Bible school graduate, felt God's call to go on an African mission outreach, but she had no money for the trip. When she and her prayer partner prayed, the friend saw a vision of two bags falling at Anne's feet with the needed two thousand dollars. Uncontrollable laughter hit Anne.

"I am going to laugh my way to Africa," she told her praying friend.

In just two days all the money came in unexpected ways—including a check for one thousand dollars. Anne later told Quin, "I laughed at the devil while I was waiting for the money, because I knew he wasn't going to steal it and keep me from going on God's mission. I also laughed with joy over what God was going to accomplish."

Anne has since served the Lord in several nations, depending entirely on his provision, which comes in unexpected ways. Every time the devil tries to discourage her by saying, "The money's not coming," she laughs out loud. "Oh yes, it is, Devil," she says. "My God shall supply all my needs." She then laughs her way to Korea or Japan or Malaysia, just as she did to Africa.

## PRAY IN AGREEMENT

As Anne's story illustrates, there is strength in numbers. The prayer of agreement can be a powerful strategy in spiritual warfare. Jesus said: "If two of you on earth agree about anything you ask for, it will be done for you by my Father in heaven. For where two or three come together in my name, there am I with them" (Mt 18:19, 20).

The word *agree* in this Scripture is from a Greek root from which we get our English word *symphony*. It means "to be in harmony or accord concerning a matter."

We find it essential to have at least one specific friend—someone familiar with the current battles we're dealing with—to stand in agreement with us as prayer support. Such partners also provide a blanket of prayer for us when we're traveling, ministering—or writing a book!

Prayer partners play a spiritual role that is analogous to the army specialists who create a "corridor of safety" for the tanks and armaments to mount an offensive against the enemy. These soldiers learn to detonate land mines, clear barbed-wire entanglements, bulldoze man-made barriers, and build emergency bridges over trenches. Only then can the army invade enemy territory and liberate the captives. Prayer partners often pray in advance to help clear the way—neutralizing the enemy's offense forces.

Individual prayer and warfare is important, but interceding with a prayer partner or a group of believers strengthens the prayer's effectiveness. If the two of you or the entire group is fasting in unity, the warfare is even stronger.

First we should ask the Lord *how* he wants us to pray.

Then in agreement, *with one mind,* we pray as he directs, persisting with our prayer partners until we see results.


## BIND THE STRONG MAN

Jesus gave us his authority over the devil and his evil cohorts, yet we must be motivated to use it if we want to see results. Consider what he taught his followers: "I will give you the keys of the kingdom of heaven; whatever you bind on earth will be bound in heaven, and whatever you loose on earth will be loosed in heaven" (Mt 16:19).

He also says, "No one can enter a strong man's house and plunder his goods, unless he first binds the strong man, and then he will plunder his house" (Mk 3:27, *NKJV*).

To bind evil spirits means to restrain them by addressing them directly and forbidding them to continue their destructive activity. Through the power of the Holy Spirit, our words loose the person from the enemy's bondage. In prayer we ask the Holy Spirit to minister to his or her need. Our prayer is directed to God, our warfare at the enemy. This tactic of binding evil spirits is especially effective when praying in agreement with a prayer partner.

Renee is a spiritual warrior who's learned to use this important tactic. One day she went to visit her nineteen-year-old son. Not finding him at home, she went on in. Horrified at the mess she found, she began to clean the apartment—straightening, dusting, sweeping, and scrubbing. She even cooked a meal, then washed all the dirty clothes lying around.

While putting things in order, Renee found a gun Mike

had stolen from her policeman husband, Mike's stepfather. It had one bullet in it. Somehow Renee knew Mike's intent was to shoot himself. She began to do spiritual battle for her son's life.

"Thank you, Lord, for giving us authority to use your name to set captives free. I plead the blood of Jesus over Mike, and ask you to protect his life.

"I come against the strong man of rejection operating against my son, and bind your power in Jesus' name. You spirit of suicide, you will not have my son. I bind all spirits of rejection, hate, anger, murder, and suicide, in Jesus' name. I bind all unclean spirits associated with drug abuse, and cut Mike loose from past hurts and from unhealthy relationships. I command the spirits that are blinding and controlling him to release him, in Jesus' name.

"Lord, let your peace permeate this apartment. Show Mike how much you love him and desire to set him free from the bondage of the enemy. Thank you, Lord, for protecting his life and drawing him into fellowship with you."

Renee sang and filled the place with praises to the Lord as she cooked and cleaned. Before leaving she posted a note: "Mike—I did this today because I love you. No strings attached. Mom."

Seven difficult years passed before Mike finally came to Renee and asked her to pray for his deliverance. At last he was set free. "If I hadn't fought for Mike and kept showing him unconditional love, I don't think my son would still be alive," Renee told me. But he is alive, and serving the Lord with his wife and children.

Sometimes the strong man that needs binding is easily discerned—for instance, fear at an auto wreck, or lust at a beer party on the beach. At other times it is less obvious. Only God can reveal the appropriate strategy.

Linda Raney Wright gives sound advice:

"Any activity in terms of spiritual fighting or warfare must be done under the leadership of the Holy Spirit. For if God has the last word concerning events that transpire in our lives, then God, alone, can show us what to do, when to do it, and how.... We must *totally* rely on the leading of the Holy Spirit and the Word of God as to the course we take in the midst of any kind of fight or opposition or problem.... If we are listening and want to follow Him, God will tell us when to fight and when to rest; when to wait and when to move.[7]

Though we live in the world, we have discovered as Paul did that we cannot wage war as the world does. Thank the Lord for the weapons and strategy he has provided, and for the indwelling Holy Spirit, who empowers us to get the job done.

# SEVEN

# An Open Door
# to the Enemy

*You shall have no other gods before me. You shall not make
yourself any graven image.... You shall not bow down
yourself to them or serve them; for I the Lord your God am
a jealous God, visiting the iniquity of the fathers upon the
children to the third and fourth generation of those who
hate Me, but showing mercy and steadfast love to a thousand generations of those who love me and keep my commandments.* **Exodus 20:3-6, TAB**

PAULINE WAS A COMPULSIVE BUYER, addicted to shopping.
She had credit cards for most major department stores
in Atlanta and used one nearly every time she went into a
store. She couldn't resist buying something—clothes, knick-
knacks, appliances, furniture, gifts. For Pauline, shopping
was more than a hobby. It took precedence over other priorities, becoming an idol. "It's how I got my kicks," she says.

When Pauline heard a Christian teacher speak on family
generational weaknesses, she suddenly realized that her father was addicted to alcohol, but she and her sister were ob-

sessive shoppers. It was a different "substance" but the same compulsive behavior pattern.

Following the teacher's suggestions, Pauline confessed her sin and asked the Lord to forgive her. Then to break the habit's control over her, she declared aloud: "Satan, you will no longer have a foothold in my life by making me greedy for things I don't need. I renounce this idol and declare the stronghold broken by the authority of Jesus Christ. Addiction to shopping will no longer control me. I recognize this bondage of generational weakness and by the blood of Jesus I sever it."

Then she prayed, "Heavenly Father, I yield to you in this area, trusting you that this bondage is removed from my life. Thank you that by the power of the Holy Spirit and according to your Word I can and will walk in obedience to you and in victory. I make you, and you only, the Lord of my life. In Jesus' name. Amen."

Pauline and her husband had several counseling sessions with their pastor. She also destroyed all her credit cards as an outward sign that she would walk in her deliverance and keep her focus on Jesus.


OUR SPIRITUAL HERITAGE

What is the origin of such compulsive-addictive behavior? What about other problems such as chronic illness, uncontrollable anger, fear of crowds, or rebellion? How is it that the enemy has access to us as Christians?

There's no pat answer. In this and the following chapter we will look at the various factors involved. But according to the Scripture quoted at the beginning of this chapter, we can find part of the answer in our family tree. God says that the serious sin of idolatry will have repercussions upon future generations. Just as our genetic heritage determines what our physical characteristics will be, so our *spiritual heritage* bears strongly on our behavioral tendencies, both positive and negative.

The iniquity of the forefathers brings a curse upon the family line. This word *iniquity* does not mean individual sinful acts; it means "perverseness" and comes from a Hebrew root meaning "to be bent or crooked."[1] The word implies a basic attitude of rebellion, plus the consequences that iniquity produces. We see the same word in the prophecy concerning Jesus the Messiah: "The Lord has laid on him the *iniquity* of us all" (Is 53:6, emphasis mine). Jesus bore the cumulative sinfulness of mankind.

We are not responsible for our forefathers' individual acts of sin; we have plenty of our own for which we are responsible. And Galatians 3:13 declares that Jesus became a curse for us, providing a means for our deliverance. But we do inherit a susceptibility to sin in the same areas that troubled our forefathers. We tend to be "bent or crooked" in the same places, as Pauline's case illustrates. Our enemy is not omniscient, but he knows where these weak areas are, because his agents have been working against our family members for generations.

We see such sin patterns in families all the time, including the families in the Bible. Look at Abraham, the patriarch we laud as a godly example. On two occasions he lied about his wife Sarah, calling her his sister. Then Abraham's son Isaac lied about his wife Rebekah, saying she was his sister. Isaac's son Jacob deceived him so he could receive the blessing due the firstborn, Esau. Jacob's sons deceived him about his son Joseph, causing him to grieve for years. The tendency to lie and deceive showed up in succeeding generations, each time causing more serious consequences.

King David's besetting sin was his adultery with Bathsheba. Sexual sin also became a problem with his sons. Finally, because his son Solomon took hundreds of foreign wives and began to worship their false gods, God took the kingdom from him. The gravity of Solomon's sin was even greater than that of his father David.

## SINS THAT BRING CURSES

We read in Deuteronomy chapters 27 and 28 that curses are promised for sins in these six areas: idolatry, dishonoring of parents, dishonesty and deception, cruelty to the helpless, sexual sin of any kind, and disregard for the law. (Some references concerning the sins of the fathers are Deuteronomy 29:24-28; 2 Chronicles 7:19-22; 34:23-25; Ezra 9:4, 13-15; Nehemiah 9:1-3; Isaiah 65:6-7; Jeremiah 14:20-22; 16:10-13.)

Pastor Burton Stokes writes:

There is that unseen and mysterious connection between a father's sins and the path of his children. If the father commits certain kinds of sin, his offspring are prone to the same kinds of sin, regardless of their training, or the social, cultural, and environmental influences on them.... Sin is committed and iniquity is "passed down" to the children, to the third and fourth generation.... Each generation adds to the cumulative iniquity, further weakening the resistance of the next generation.[2]

We do not mean to imply that there is any deficiency in the power of the blood of Jesus, which redeems us from the curse of sin, or that believers today are bound to the letter of Old Testament law. But if we rebel in our hearts and rebuild idols in our lives, we can be ensnared again by the same yoke of bondage from which we've been delivered (see Gal 5:1, 16). Thus we again become susceptible to the curse.

Bible teacher Derek Prince writes:

Sometimes curses may not have their origin in previous generations. They may be the result of deeds or events in your own lifetime. Or it may be that a curse from previous generations has been compounded by things you yourself have done.... Christians who are undisciplined, disobedient, and out of harmony forfeit their claim on God's protection.[3]

These insights are not intended to bring us into fear or bondage, nor cause us to attribute every problem, habit, or bad character trait to a curse or a demon. Emotional and behavioral problems sometimes have a physiological or biological base. For instance, premenstrual women often have fluctuating blood sugar levels that trigger and intensify symptoms such as exhaustion, depression, anxiety, irritability, headaches, dizziness, and mood swings. And menopause sometimes causes the same symptoms, in addition to annoying hot flashes. Certainly prayer is always appropriate, but some of these problems may also call for treatment by diet modification, hormone supplements, or vitamin therapy. Ask the Lord for guidance in these matters.

Looking at various issues we've discussed in this chapter helps us to become aware of our vulnerabilities, to renounce the sins we've yielded to in our areas of weakness, and then with the help of the Holy Spirit to strengthen our defenses against the evil one.

You may wish to pray like this: "Father, I come before you as Daniel did to confess and repent of my sin and the iniquity of my forefathers. Forgive us for the sins of idolatry, witchcraft, rebellion, immorality of any kind, and all addictions. [Add anything the Holy Spirit prompts you to include.]

"According to Ephesians 6:12, I bind all principalities and powers trying to influence me or my family, and I forbid them to operate in the name of Jesus. I declare that this family is under the blood of Jesus; I revoke any generational curses and say they will go no further. Jesus became a curse for us, and we are a generation that serves God.

"Father, forgive us for depending upon any source besides you for peace and fulfillment. Pour out your supernatural power in my family, so we will not be bound by the things of the natural world. I ask you to send warrior angels to do battle on our behalf. Thank you that my children will take their place in the body of Christ and fulfill your calling upon their lives.

"Father, I submit to you, and my hope and expectations are from you alone (Ps 62:5, TAB). By the power and authority of Jesus Christ of Nazareth, I declare *any* satanic influence directed toward me or my family defeated by Jesus' death on the cross.

"Thank you for freeing us from the bondage of our past and cleansing us by the blood of Christ. Thank you for our positive heritage—for those ancestors who did follow you and prayed for us. Thank you for your mercy and for the blessings you bestow upon me and my family. Amen."

## THE DANGER OF IDOLATRY

Though God strictly forbade Israel to engage in any form of idol worship, his people rebelled against him. They committed spiritual adultery as they took up their neighbors' evil ways of idolatry. As a result God removed his protection, allowing these enemies to capture and enslave them. McCandlish Phillips explains the gravity of this sin:

> Satan lusts for worship. Because it belongs exclusively to God, he desires it for himself. He would rather have worship than anything else.... He sets up many objects as alternatives to the worship of God. This is idolatry in the crudest form.
> ... Satan stands behind every image and every idol, receiving as unto himself the worship, the respect, and adoration that is directed to them, which belongs only to the living God.... The cumulative effect of idols and images is to bring a curse upon the land.[4]

Ruthanne and her husband have observed in their overseas travel that the areas of the world filled with idols and false religions are generally among the poorest and most disease-ridden nations on earth. They're more keenly aware of the need for God's protection when they travel in those areas. Ruthanne shares some examples.

## PROTECTED BY THE BLOOD OF JESUS

Once on a ministry trip to India our intended host had become ill, so we stayed with a family who were nominal Christians. Hideous images of Hindu gods decorated the walls of our room, but we were too blurry from jet lag and thirty-six hours of travel to give them more than a passing glance as we fell into bed. In the middle of the night fireworks celebrating a Hindu festival awakened us. A sudden wave of nausea swept over me, and my head throbbed with pain. Sensing an evil presence in the room emanating from those images, I began to bind the spirits of bondage, oppression, and Antichrist, and to plead the blood of Jesus over myself.

My husband commanded all evil spirits to leave, then he prayed for my healing. For the next five hours we played tapes of praise and worship. We dedicated the room to God for the week of our visit. I rested and recuperated the next day, then was able to keep my speaking engagement.

I don't believe our host family gave credence to those images; they just considered them a part of the room's decor. But the images gave the evil spirits a legal right to be present until we drove them away. In fact, the artisans who make such objects often do their work under demonic influence, and they invite the evil spirits to inhabit the objects. I believe I was vulnerable to attack because of fatigue and I wasn't alert and attentive to the Holy Spirit.

We had a similar experience in Bali, Indonesia. The boy who cleaned our hotel room every day gave us a carved figure as a gift on the day we left. We accepted it graciously and gave him the customary tip for his services. After arriving at our next stop, both of us began having physical problems, and we suspected it had to do with that little statue. We learned it was the image of a Hindu god. When we got rid of it, we both recovered!

People in Western cultures rarely bow down to images or idols, although the influx of New Age and Eastern religious practices has made it more prevalent in recent years. But many New Testament references to idolatry equate this sin with rebellion, infidelity, immorality, and other sins of the flesh (see Col 3:5; Rom 1:22-25; Gal 4:8-9). *Nelson's Illustrated Bible Dictionary* says:

> In the New Testament period... idolatry became not the actual bowing down before a statue but the replacement of God in the mind of the worshiper.... The modern believer must understand the vicious nature of idolatry. While we may not make or bow down to a statue, we must be constantly on guard that we let nothing come between us and God. As soon as anything does, that thing is an idol.
>
> In addition to material objects such as houses, land, and cars, idols can be people, popular heroes, or those whom we love. Objects of worship can even include things like fame, reputation, hobbies, pride, and deeds done in the name of the Lord. Idolatry is a dangerous and deceitful sin.[5]

## CAN A CHRISTIAN HAVE A DEMON?

Perhaps no other question has generated more debate and disagreement among Christians.

We firmly believe a Christian who is walking in right relationship to God cannot be possessed by a demon. That would imply ownership or total control, and a Christian belongs to Christ, not the devil. But a believer who has compromised with the enemy—who has fallen into idolatry and removed himself from God's protection—can certainly be tormented, harassed, or open to deception by demonic forces.

Dr. Ed Murphy, Bible school teacher and former missionary, writes:

> Satan's goal is, through deception, to entice believers to sin or commit any act which quenches the Holy Spirit in their lives and/or to lessen their effectiveness in glorifying God through both personal conduct and Christian service. His desire is to find any area of our lives to which he can attach himself (Eph 4:27). Through his demons he seeks to find any *sin handles* which give him the right to influence us into actions of disobedience to God. Satan was unsuccessful in his attempts to do so with the man Christ Jesus. He did, however, have success in the life of the apostle Peter (Lk 22:31-34). And he continues to be successful in the lives of many believers.
>
> Paul warned the Corinthians of the satanic dimension of sexual temptation (1 Cor 7:5). He also expressed his fear that Satan would be successful in drawing the

Thessalonian believers away from a life of obedience to God (1 Thes 3:5).[6]

To the degree we choose to obey God—allowing the Holy Spirit to renew our minds through God's Word—to that degree we can overcome Satan's efforts to ensnare us!

Consider Peter, who after hearing Jesus say he would be killed and then raised on the third day, declared, "Never, Lord!... This shall never happen to you!"

"Get behind me, Satan!" Jesus responded. "You are a stumbling block to me; you do not have in mind the things of God, but the things of men" (Mt 16:22-23).

Peter had walked with the Lord all of his ministry years. Yet Jesus indicated Satan was influencing this disciple to focus on what he wanted, not on God's plan. His perspective was both limited and selfish, as ours often is. We can be thankful that Peter's will did not prevail!

Then we read of Simon the sorcerer, who became a Christian under Philip's ministry in Samaria (Acts 8:5-23). "Simon himself believed... and after being baptized devoted himself constantly to him [Philip]" (v. 13, *TAB*). Later, when Peter and other apostles laid hands on the new converts and they received the Holy Spirit, Simon was impressed. He offered to pay them to give him that power.

"Your heart is all wrong in God's sight," Peter told him. "For I see that you are in the gall of bitterness and a bond forged by iniquity" (Acts 8:21, 23, *TAB*). Although Simon had become a Christian, the bond to his occult past had not been broken. He yielded to Satan's influence upon his mind, and he sought a way to draw acclaim to himself, as he had done before his conversion (see Acts 8:10, 11). Fortunately, Simon received Peter's rebuke and asked him to pray for him.

What about Judas? For three years he associated closely with Jesus almost daily. Yet Satan entered his heart and caused him to betray the Master (see Jn 13:21-27).

## DOORS TO THE DEMONIC

Dr. Murphy explains the meaning of Christians being demonized: "By demonization I mean that Satan, through his evil spirits, exercises direct partial control over one or more areas of the life of a human being."[7]

He also suggests there are three main doors through which demons enter a human life:

The first door is *at birth*. Some Christians were born demonized. This is often called by different names such as generational sin, familial sin, demonic transference, demonic inheritance, or the law of the inheritance of evil.

The second door to demonize Christians is *through child abuse*, in at least four possible areas—sexual, physical, psychological, and spiritual.

Spiritual child abuse... can occur when a child involuntarily receives demonic psychic/occult powers that are passed down through the family line. It can also occur when a child is voluntarily subjected to a spirit ceremony with the purpose of passing demonic psychic or occult spirits into his body. It can also occur when a curse is placed on a child by a malevolent spiritual practitioner, or by an angry person operating in the spirit realm.

... The third door... is through his or her own *willful sinful actions* in childhood, youth, or adulthood. This usually occurs in the realms of sexuality, occult, and destructive interpersonal relationships.

Sin has been the scourge of humanity since the Fall. With sin comes demons.... Increased demonic activity and increased sinfulness go together.[8]

## LONGING TO BE FREE

In ministering to hundreds of people all over the world, we have seen countless examples of believers under demonic bondage to one degree or another. Many, until they receive teaching on this subject, are unable even to identify their problem clearly. They just know something is wrong. And they long to be free.

After Quin had been teaching a Christian women's group how to pray for their families, a woman asked for prayer.

"If there's anything in me that is blocking prayer—and there must be because my prayer life is so lacking—I want to be free," she whispered.

I studied the woman's face and noticed a strange stare in her eyes.

"Is Jesus Christ your personal Lord?" I asked.

"Yes, for over ten years," she nodded. "I love him."

The Holy Spirit prompted me to ask, "Do you have an American Indian heritage? Or do you think a curse could have been sent against you?"

"My granddaddy was an Indian chief," she answered.

Before I could even begin to pray she suddenly spun into an Indian dance, complete with war whoops and shrieks. I was numb with shock for a few moments; I'd never encountered such a demonic manifestation. Then several of us gathered around her and began singing about the blood of Jesus.

Taking authority in the name of Jesus, we commanded the evil spirits to be silent. In moments the woman quieted down and began responding to our prayers. She declared any curses against her to be null and void by the power of Jesus Christ. She asked God's forgiveness for the sins of her forefathers and for her own sin, and ordered all unclean spirits to depart, never to torment her again.

"I don't know exactly what happened to me tonight, but I feel so free," she said, smiling, after our prayer session. Some of the leaders in the group agreed to follow up and help her walk in her deliverance.

I can't say whether curses were said over her as a child growing up in her Indian family, whether a relative had dedicated her to a false god when she was a baby, or whether she herself had opened the door for evil spirits to torment her. I can only report what happened that night when she was released from bondage to freely worship the Lord Jesus Christ, and her whole countenance changed before our eyes.

## ASK FOR DISCERNMENT

When the Lord brings to my attention things from my past which need to be addressed spiritually, I renounce all generational sin and appropriate the cleansing blood of Jesus. Once while visiting in Virginia I stood on the spot where General Robert E. Lee surrendered to General U.S. Grant to end our nation's Civil War. I remitted the sins of my slave-owning great-great grandparents and asked God's forgiveness for all prejudice in our family.

On a visit to Germany I felt led to remit the sins of my husband's forefathers, since my children carry an inheritance from those ancestors. I've renounced divorce, infidelity, membership in secret societies, and other generational weaknesses as they've been revealed. With Nehemiah I've said, "I and my father's house have sinned" (Neh 1:6b, *NAS*). But I thank God for his forgiveness through the shed blood of Jesus our Savior. My husband and I and our children don't have to live under guilt, condemnation, or fear. "So if the Son sets you free, you will be free indeed" (Jn 8:36).

Why address this issue of doors being opened to the enemy? To help women overcome generational weaknesses and iniquities, break the cycles of bondage in themselves and in their children, and make their homes a spiritual refuge. Then they can move on to fulfill God's purposes for their lives and become effective in spiritual warfare. Pauline, the addicted shopper, is just one of many we've interviewed who has been set free.

Next we look at how to find the areas where doors have been opened to the enemy, and provide guidelines for closing them.

# EIGHT

# Breaking Bondages

*It is for freedom that Christ has set us free. Stand firm, then, and do not let yourselves be burdened again by a yoke of slavery.* **Galatians 5:1**

ELLEN HAD BEEN A CHRISTIAN since childhood, but when things didn't go her way, she verbally attacked those who displeased her. She excused her temper by saying, "Well after all, I'm Irish, and everyone knows the Irish easily fly off the handle."

That was Ellen's particular negative spiritual heritage (not to imply that all Irish persons are short-tempered). It was a vulnerable area where the enemy took advantage. And becoming a Christian didn't eradicate her bad temper. She just made excuses for it.

When the Lord spotlighted her problem, Ellen repented, renounced her sin of anger and speaking bitter words, and declared the bondage broken by the blood of Jesus.

"I had to see my anger for what it was; bondage to sin that was rooted in unforgiveness," she said. "Then I asked the Holy Spirit to alert me when I'm in danger of falling into the old habit." Ellen walks in an attitude of forgiveness and renews her mind with Scripture to keep the enemy from ensnaring her again.

## CHAINS TO THE PAST

Untold numbers of believers struggle with problems like Ellen's that paralyze their spiritual growth. Such bondage or enslavement is like a chain holding us tightly to our past—to an area of weakness from our pre-Christian experience or to a vulnerable area from our negative spiritual heritage. It exists because a door has been opened, and we have given the enemy the right to enter. These bondages usually affect our mind, will, and emotions. They in turn influence our behavior: outbursts of anger, rebellion, depression, threats of suicide, compulsive eating, lying, stealing, sexual sin, substance addictions, destructive behavior, and so on.

The apostle Paul addressed this problem in writing to the church at Corinth: "I fear that there may be quarreling, jealousy, outbursts of anger, factions, slander, gossip, arrogance and disorder. I am afraid that when I come again my God will humble me before you, and I will be grieved over many who have sinned earlier and have not repented of the impurity, sexual sin, and debauchery in which they have indulged" (2 Cor 12:20b, 21).

Many Christians struggling with these problems are leading defeated lives, burdened with guilt. They try to change their behavior on their own, only to fail and sink deeper into despair. They must be cut free from the chains that hold them.

We examine some major areas of bondage in this chapter:

- unforgiveness
- grief and disappointment
- addictions
- rejection and a negative self-image
- illicit sexual activity
- occult involvement.

## UNFORGIVENESS

Children in their naivete sometimes express profound truth in the simplest of words—or even made-up words. Ruthanne's husband came home from a weekend preaching trip recently and shared a new version of the Lord's Prayer from a pastor's young son: "Forgive us our trash-passes, as we forgive those who pass trash against us.... "

To forgive means to give up the desire to get even or to "pass trash" against someone. It means to renounce anger and resentment, to release one's debtor. It is a decision made with the will. We can *decide* to forgive the person who has offended us, whether we feel like it or not.[1]

We put forgiveness in its proper perspective when we realize that any injustice we have suffered from another person is small compared to our own sin against God. In other words, the "trash" we've passed against our loving heavenly Father is much worse than all the "trash" others have passed against us!

The Lord's command is quite explicit: "If you forgive men when they sin against you, your heavenly Father will also forgive you. But if you do not forgive men their sins, your

Father will not forgive your sins" (Mt 6:14).

Paul says, "Get rid of all bitterness, rage and anger, brawling and slander, along with every form of malice. Be kind and compassionate to one another, forgiving each other, just as in Christ God forgave you" (Eph 4:31, 32). He writes to the Corinthians: "I have forgiven in the sight of Christ for your sake, in order that Satan might not outwit us. For we are not unaware of his schemes" (2 Cor 2:10b, 11).

We are *required* to forgive if we want God to forgive us. Gratitude for the mercy God extends to us, and a desire to demonstrate that gratitude by obeying his Word, helps us to forgive our offenders. When we recall Jesus' plea as he hung on the cross; "Father, forgive them, for they do not know what they are doing" (Lk 23:34), we are faced with our own sin and the need to free others by forgiving them.


WOUNDED PRIDE

Unforgiveness creates a bondage between the person who suffered the offense and the person who caused it. With forgiveness it is broken, both parties are released, and the Holy Spirit can then bring healing and restoration. In fact, a positive bonding in God's love can then take place. Beverly's story is an example.

Beverly's pride suffered a blow when her daughter Rena got a divorce, but when she learned Rena was pregnant by her latest boyfriend she was furious. For days she struggled with her anger and disappointment. Then she agonized with guilt, knowing she ought to forgive because she was a Christian.

"I felt the enemy was stealing the very life from our family: my husband was angry, my daughter was ashamed, and I had so much pride I didn't want an illegitimate baby to come into our lives," said Beverly. "I knew I had to attack the situation with spiritual warfare, and that forgiveness was the key.

"First, I told Rena face-to-face that I was disappointed by her actions but that I chose to forgive her. Then I asked God to forgive me for my anger, pride, and selfish attitude.

"I entered into battle and declared, 'Satan, I don't care what you try to do to us as a family. God's love and God's hold on us is far greater than anything you can do. Your attack is broken in Jesus' name, and God will help us walk through this and stand together. The twenty-one years I have invested in my daughter are not going to be lost over this one incident.'"

Beverly then prayed, "God, I release myself totally to you—whatever your plan is for me as a grandmother. I ask you to minister to Rena, draw her heart toward you, and knit us together in your love. Please bring this baby safely into the world. Thank you that it will be a blessing to all of us."

Beverly's bondage was broken when she forgave her daughter, and eventually the negative emotions stopped tormenting her. Rena is now going to college, and she and her baby are living with Beverly and her husband. The Lord is helping them restore a relationship based on his love.


## GRIEF: A PROCESS

Solomon wrote, "... heartache crushes the spirit.... A crushed spirit dries up the bones" (Prv 15:13; 17:22).

Grief comes through many causes: a broken relationship,

loss of a loved one, a business, a job, or broken dreams. It may come through a miscarriage or barrenness, or through disappointment in yourself or another person. We can even be disappointed by God, feeling that he let us down when we needed him.

Victims of grief are prone to get on the "If only... " treadmill and lament their own failure: "If only I'd made her stay at home, that drunk driver wouldn't have killed my daughter. She would be alive today." The enemy uses such tactics to produce guilt and despair, which often lead to anger against God.

Grieving should follow a natural process over a reasonable time span, which psychologists say normally ranges from one to three years. It is a process of healing. But unresolved, prolonged grief opens the door to spiritual, physical, and emotional problems and a bondage that paralyzes spiritual progress.

In order to be free, the grief-stricken person must eventually be able to release her disappointment and say, "God, I don't understand this tragedy, but I choose to believe that you love me, and I put my trust in you." God can then pour out the "oil of gladness instead of mourning" (Is 61:3).

Marlene and Brian reached that place of release after a rare form of influenza claimed their eight-month-old son, Neil. His birth had been hailed as a "miracle" because Marlene was supposedly barren; then suddenly he was gone. At first they felt disappointment that God had let them down. Then they thought they must have somehow failed God by not doing more to save their baby.

"As we worked through our sorrow, we derived our greatest comfort from Scripture and from Christian friends,"

Marlene said. "Finally we were able to rest in God's sovereignty, knowing our son was in his hands. On his grave marker we inscribed, 'You shall not delay to offer the first of your ripe produce.... The firstborn of your sons you shall give to Me' " (Ex 22:29, *NKJV*).

Marlene and Brian eventually went overseas to work with a children's hospital, where they touched many youngsters with God's love. "Several children died while we were there, and I was able to identify with the mothers and comfort them," Marlene said. "I had two miscarriages after losing Neil, but God was our strength through it all."

Seven years after their baby's death, while on missionary furlough, a lawyer friend arranged for them to adopt the yet unborn child of a teenager. Not only did this prevent an abortion, but Marlene and her husband were thrilled at last to have a son. Today they are in charge of a Bible school training young people for Christian ministry in Third-World countries.

## ADDICTIONS

Elizabeth goes to the beauty salon at least four times a week to maintain her impeccable appearance. Betty's addiction is sensual TV soap operas, while Faith's is the neighborhood spa. For Rhoda, keeping a meticulous house takes priority over her husband and children. Martha is a closet alcoholic, and Caroline is hooked on prescription drugs. All of these women show signs of addictive behavior.

Webster says that to be an addict means "to devote or surrender oneself to something... obsessively." The great danger of addiction is the matter of surrender—handing oneself over to another power and allowing the will to become passive. Most addicts deny that they've surrendered, insisting, "I can stop any time I want to!" But the chains hold them until they become willing to submit to the power of the Holy Spirit to be released.

Scripture warns us, "Abstain from the sensual urges—the evil desires, the passions of the flesh (your lower nature) that wage war against your soul" (1 Pt 2:11, TAB).

Caroline was in church every Sunday with her husband and two small children, seemingly a model wife and mother. But for ten years she was addicted to prescription drugs and wine. She worked as a nurse and had no trouble getting doctors to write prescriptions for her—mainly for weight loss.

"I knew I shouldn't do it," she said. "Often when I popped a pill I'd cry out, 'God, help me.' But I couldn't control myself. I knew I wasn't the mother I needed to be, but I liked the feeling, the 'high' the drugs gave me. I did it for an escape. After taking pills I'd drink wine to help me feel calm inside."

One day her sister-in-law came to see her, and during the visit shared how she talked to God. "I'd like to talk to God like that too," Caroline thought. A few days later she met a missionary who challenged her to ask Jesus to become Lord of her life. Caroline received the Lord into her heart but she continued popping pills and drinking. One day she was shocked to read in the Bible that her body is the temple of the Holy Spirit (1 Cor 3:16, 17).

She prayed, "Lord, if your Spirit is in me, and I am your temple, I don't want to abuse something so sacred. Please help me stop taking these pills."

Determined to be set free from the bondage of drugs, she went through the purses in her closet and got out all the pill bottles she'd stashed away. That night she flushed over a thousand pills down the toilet, never to take another one. And she had no withdrawal symptoms.

Three weeks later, while sipping wine one evening, she heard a voice say, "That will be the last drink, Caroline." She looked around and saw no one. Believing it was the Lord, she knew she had to chuck the wine too. She poured it all down the sink and never craved it again. God's power had broken her bondage!

Caroline has been free of drugs and alcohol for more than fifteen years. Best of all, she has a close personal relationship with Jesus. Today she is a strong intercessor for her family, community, and nation.

## THE SPIRITUAL ROOTS OF ADDICTION

Addictions—whether to drugs, alcohol, rock music, self-gratification, pornography, perfectionism, or negativism—usually stem from a desire to escape painful or difficult circumstances. But of course the addiction only makes the circumstances worse. Christian psychologist Dr. Archibald Hart writes:

All addictions have spiritual roots. Human nature is inherently rebellious and selfish. It desires self-aggrandizement and self-satisfaction. Addictions are a direct reflection and outcome of our life of bondage to this rebellion— traditionally called sin. No healing is complete, as I have repeatedly said in this book, that does not address and remove this bondage.

But addictions not only have spiritual *causes;* they have spiritual *consequences.* There are many ways in which addictions can be spiritually destructive:

- They are forms of spiritual idolatry....
- They sap energy and demand attention....
- They create a false barrier between the addict and God....
- They prevent obedience to God....
- They perpetuate sin.[2]

Often a person is driven to addictive behavior because of abuses in childhood, rape, rejection, a negative self-image, unforgiveness, guilt, or grief. If addictive patterns are in the family line, that susceptibility should be taken into account and dealt with. Ask the Holy Spirit to show you the root cause of the addiction—either your own or of the person you're praying with—and seek healing and deliverance in that area.

This can be a long, hard road. Addictions are not always broken as instantaneously as Caroline's was Addicts can struggle for years to overcome their compulsions. Christian counseling and Christian support groups are helpful for some. Victory comes by persevering in prayer, willingness to accept help from others, and hanging on to God's mercy. If we *will* to be free, we can break the bond of addiction by the power of the blood of Jesus, then walk in the Spirit (see Gal 5:16-26).

## REJECTION AND NEGATIVE SELF-IMAGE

Words, ours or others', have the power to wound or to heal the spirit. One survey indicates it takes at least five positive statements of affirmation to counteract the effects of one negative comment made to an individual. "The tongue that brings healing is a tree of life, but a deceitful tongue crushes the spirit.... The tongue has the power of life and death (Prv 15:4; 18:21).

Quin once prayed with an attractive woman in her forties who had the mistaken idea she was fat and ugly. She grew up in a rural area, and whenever her family drove past a farm with pigs, her mother would teasingly say, "Look at all the little Deenas out there. Watch them eat!"

Wounded by her mother's words, Deena struggled with a "fat" image all her life. We revoked and broke that "word curse" during a time of spiritual warfare and prayer. Then we declared that she was God's workmanship created for his glory, and we thanked the Lord that he had made Deena in his image. She was released from that bondage and is now able to see herself in a new light.

Rosa discovered the power of a "word curse" when Robert, her fifth-grader, came home with a low grade on his semester's work. The teacher wrote that she was giving him this grade because he was capable of doing much better.

"When I prayed about it, the Lord reminded me of words spoken by my mother-in-law when he was six months old," Rosa told us. "I'd completely forgotten the day she became angry with my husband when he asked her to not be so hard on her thirteen-year-old daughter. He hadn't asked her with the right attitude. Reacting angrily, his mother said, 'Wait 'til Robert's older. You'll find out what it's like not to be able to handle a kid in school!'"

Rosa recalled the Scripture: "No weapon forged against you will prevail, and you will refute every tongue that accuses you. This is the heritage of the servants of the LORD" (Is 54:17). Using that in her son's situation, she prayed and broke the words his grandmother had spoken over Robert so many years ago. His grades improved immediately, and soon he was chosen as one of two students in his class to appear on a television program because of his high learning ability. To Rosa it was confirmation that the word curse was broken.

## ILLICIT SEXUAL ACTIVITY

"Do you not know that he who unites himself with a prostitute is one with her in body? For it is said, 'The two will become one flesh.'. . . Flee from sexual immorality.... He who sins sexually sins against his own body" (1 Cor 6:16, 18).

Any sexual activity outside marriage—be it heterosexual, homosexual, child abuse, self abuse, bestiality, or whatever—is sinful, and God's people are continually warned against it. The current epidemic of sexually transmitted diseases bears out Paul's warning: "For the wages of sin is death, but the gift of God is eternal life in Christ Jesus our Lord" (Rom 6:23). Where sexual sin is concerned the wages can be physical, spiritual, or emotional death. This type of sin can also open the door to demonic influences.

A victim of incest or rape, though she didn't willingly engage in the sexual activity, is nevertheless held by an invisible chain to her aggressor. It can affect her relationship with God and with other people, her emotions, and her self-image. Forgiving the aggressor is the key to deliverance, but intensive counseling often is needed.[3]

A frequent result of sexual sin is abortion. Pro-life supporters insist that abortion-on-demand has serious spiritual consequences, both for the woman who chooses it and for our nation that has legalized it. The testimony of an anonymous writer who underwent two abortions—the second one after having become a Christian—supports the claim.

## SPIRITS OF DEATH

"Satan oppresses these women, injecting thoughts into their minds," she writes. "He bombards them with guilt, condemnation, remorse, self-justification, self-loathing, self-hate, and suicidal thoughts. Evil spirits often come through the spiritual door that the abortion has opened to the enemy—spirits from which the woman must be delivered."[4]

Following an abortion at age twenty, this young woman, a traditional churchgoer, committed her life to Christ. She began studying to become a missionary doctor. But later while in medical school she dated a backslidden Christian and became pregnant again. Her boyfriend didn't want the baby, and she was unwilling to abandon her educational goals. So she had a second abortion. But this time the aftermath was more intense.

"How ironic it all was," she observes. "I was willing to lie, cheat, and kill in order to 'work for Jesus.' Next to my personal goals, my child's life was not important. Such a selfish agenda almost cost me my life and sanity."[5]

She repented and received God's forgiveness, but could not forgive herself.

"This unforgiveness allowed evil spirits a foothold," she continues. "A spirit of suicide—a murderous spirit directed inward—had a stronghold in my life. I was so oppressed by the spirit that I could actually hear the demons sing to me: 'Wanna die, wanna die, wanna die!' This went on for many weeks."[6]

Her deliverance came when God spoke to her in church through this Scripture: "I will not die but live, and will proclaim what the LORD has done. The LORD has chastened me severely, but he has not given me over to death. Open for me the gates of righteousness; I will enter and give thanks to the LORD" (Ps 118:17-19).

"I realized that I had a choice," she writes. "I didn't have to die! I could live! Those suicidal thoughts were the devil talking to me.

"I went home preparing to do war. I pushed my front door open and spoke to the enemy as I walked in: 'This is it, Devil!' I studied Psalm 118:17-19 and Isaiah 38:18-19. I forgave myself, and I forgave the men in my life who had hurt me. Then I prepared for bed.

"It was completely dark in my bedroom. My curtains were so thick that no light came in from the street as I got in bed. I remember praying, and then I saw three rust-colored beings appear on my ceiling. I told them: 'I'm going to live and not die, so I can declare the works of the Lord. The living will praise him. Death cannot praise the Lord; the grave cannot celebrate him. Those who go down into the pit cannot hope for his truth. I'm going to live, and I'm not going to die! Get out, and don't ever come back again, in the name of Jesus.'"

She said those last words again, and the evil beings disappeared.

"Because of God's mercy, I am still alive. The Lord has chastened me, but he has not given me over to death. Now I am completely free from that spirit of suicide, and I endeavor to live a life that honors the Lord."[7]

## OCCULT INVOLVEMENT

Deuteronomy 18:9-14 declares that occult activity is an abomination to God. Such activity includes astrology (reading horoscopes), palm reading, Ouija boards, Tarot cards, seances, fortune-telling, witchcraft, divination, sorcery, magic, casting spells or hexes, secret societies, and more.

An amazing number of Christians expose themselves to demonic activity by going to a fortune-teller. They often laugh it off by saying, "Oh, but I didn't take it seriously." That doesn't change the fact that God's Word speaks against it. And evil spirits *do* take it seriously.

Others innocently purchase or accept as gifts objects that have occult significance. I, Quin, have personally done a thorough housecleaning of such objects. I began by going from room to room in my house and asking, "Lord Jesus, is there anything in here that is an abomination to you? Anything that's connected with the occult or the demonic realm?"

I got rid of face masks from the West Indies, Greek souvenirs with mythical goddesses on them, a world map with astrological signs around it, an Indian painting and other wall hangings that missionary friends told me had Hindu deities on them. I even found some souvenir dishes given me that had pictures of Roman gods painted on them. Out they went.

God's warning to the Israelites is as appropriate for us today as then: "The images of their gods you are to burn in the fire. Do not covet the silver and gold on them, and do not take it for yourselves, or you will be ensnared by it" (Dt 7:25).

A friend of mine finally got free of depression after she and her prayer partner burned a stack of comic books that her husband had been collecting for eight years as a "future investment." Satanic and New Age teachings filled their pages, and my friend, a committed Christian, had had no peace since he'd started bringing them home.

"It took over an hour for them to burn—it was really eerie," she told me. "A strong wind came up, and we had to pray the nearby forest wouldn't catch fire when the ashes began blowing. It was as if those books just didn't want to be destroyed. But when they were gone, I had no more depression and my husband was so relieved, he was glad he'd agreed to let me burn them."

When Paul preached the gospel in Ephesus, the converts got rid of all their occult books: "Many also of those who were now believers came making full confession and thoroughly exposing their [former deceptive and evil] practices. And many of those who had practiced curious magical arts collected their books and (throwing them book after book on the pile) burned them in the sight of everybody. When they counted the value of them, they found it amounted to fifty thousand pieces of silver" (Acts 19:18, 19, *TAB*).

## WALKING FREE

The bondages described in this chapter frequently entangle God's children and render them powerless in spiritual warfare. If the devil cannot get you to renounce your faith altogether, he will try to ensnare you with these traps and make you ineffective. Let us look at the steps we can take in order to walk free:

1. Identify the problem area. Ask the Holy Spirit to show you any areas of bondage you may have overlooked.
2. Confess and repent before the Lord the sins the Holy Spirit reveals to you.
3. Choose to forgive all who have wounded you; also forgive yourself. Release your anger toward God, your feeling that he "let you down."
4. Receive God's forgiveness and cleansing.
5. Renounce the sin and close the door in any area where the enemy has gained entry.
6. Ask the Holy Spirit to help you break the behavior and thought patterns you've become accustomed to (see Phil 4:7-9).
7. Allow the Holy Spirit to daily conform you to the image of Christ.

## A Prayer for Walking Free

"Father, thank you for shining the light of the Holy Spirit into my heart and revealing to me the areas of bondage where I need deliverance. Lord Jesus, pride is not going to keep me from receiving your healing and freedom. I humble myself and confess my sins of rebellion. [Name the areas of sin you wish to confess. Speak out what the Holy Spirit reveals.]

"I renounce the sin of _____ and declare it will no longer have dominion over me. I close all doors where the enemy has gained entry, and I ask you to seal these areas with the blood of Jesus. Holy Spirit, please help me to focus my thoughts on the things of God and break my old patterns of thinking and acting.

"Father, I forgive _____ for wounding me. I release [him] from all judgment so that you can minister to [his] deepest need, and I release my disappointment in you because this happened. I choose to obey your Word which says, 'Get rid of all bitterness, rage and anger, brawling and slander, along with every form of malice' (Eph 4:31). Thank you, Lord, for cleansing me from all sin.

"Thank you, Lord, that I am called to freedom and not to slavery, and that I will not be ensnared again with a yoke of bondage (Gal 5:1, 13). I *will* walk in my freedom, in the mighty name of Jesus. Amen!"

# NINE

# Fight for Your Children

*Don't be afraid of them [your enemies]. Remember the
Lord, who is great and awesome, and fight for... your sons
and your daughters.* **Nehemiah 4:14**

A LL HER CLOTHING WAS BLACK, except for a white turtle-
neck splashed with prints of skulls and crossbones. As
she scooted by to claim her airplane seat, Ruthanne was
shocked to see that under her long hair one side of her head
had been shaved. Her silver jewelry depicted various
witchcraft symbols. Pasty-looking makeup, heavy eyeliner
and mascara, and dark red lipstick spoiled her youthful
good looks.

"She can't be more than sixteen," I thought to myself. "I
wonder if she's caught up in the witchcraft fad going
around."

Her chatter revealed that she was just a typical youngster
going to Canada to visit relatives over spring break. "My
mom's afraid I'll have trouble going through immigration,"
she said to the young man beside her, nervously brushing
her hair to camouflage the baldness.

"Lord, she's so young and naive, with no idea of the danger she could be getting involved in," I began to pray silently. "Father, please reveal your truth to her. Have someone witness to her. Give her mother the wisdom to know how to deal with this situation."

## A BATTLE IN THE CLASSROOM

Though many parents seem almost unaware of it, a battle is raging today to win the allegiance of our children—kids like that youngster I saw on the plane. We see Satan's influence in all these areas that have a part in molding the leaders of tomorrow:

- curricular materials in public schools
- commercial toys and video games
- cartoons, TV shows, and movies
- children's literature and comic books
- secular music, rap groups, and MTVs
- fashion trends and hairstyles
- even cereal box graphics!

Our cherished Christian values are rapidly being replaced with a "do-it-yourself" sort of religion called New Age. It's actually a blend of Western atheistic humanism and Eastern mysticism. Not new at all, but very dangerous. And its proponents have high on their list of objectives the indoctrination of our children and youth.

In her book *Like Lambs to the Slaughter*, Johanna Michaelson gives this description of New Age values:

Some cling to pyramids, crystals, channelers, goddess-worship, meditation, and guided imagery. Other New Agers are into the political aspects of globalism, saving the environment, "human potential," or any combination of the above. All, however, would agree that "dogma" and "decalogues" are out.... The New Age is the ultimate eclectic religion of self: Whatever *you* decide is right for you is what's right, as long as you don't get narrow-minded and exclusive about it.

... In growing numbers of schools around the country, the children are being taught how to contact their spirit guides (euphemistically called their "Higher Self" or their "Inner Wisdom") to help them solve problems. They are being sent home with assignments to research their astrological sign or to draw a *mandala* [a graphic symbol used in meditation] for art class or to practice the exciting rituals which little Elizabeth and Jennifer and Amanda do in some very popular children's books in order to become initiated into Witchcraft.[1]

## WHO WRITES THE BOOKS?

For many years humanist-oriented educators have been proclaiming their philosophy in the public schools through curricular programs they call "values clarification." Their goal is to neutralize, then eradicate, a basic Judeo-Christian view parents tend to assume the public schools support. Textbook researcher Mel Gabler shares his insight:

The wording of many texts is designed to first sow seeds

of doubt in the student's mind concerning his present values. Gradually he reaches the position of not believing anything; then the texts subtly indoctrinate the student with new "values," such as anti-Americanism, hatred for the home and family, man as an animal, and anti-Christian attitudes.[2]

An alarming number of curricular programs instruct teachers in how to lead pupils in occult activity. The *Impressions* Series for kindergarten through grade eight (distributed by Harcourt Brace Jovanovich) is one of the worst offenders. Mel Gabler writes that parents' complaints about this series include these observations:

- obsession with witches, ghosts, black cats, chants, spells, magic goblins, spirits, and other aspects of the occult
- undermining authority figures such as parents
- attacks on traditional families
- repeated themes of evil
- recurrent despair, gloom, hopelessness, revenge, violence, manipulation, nightmares, and anxiety
- much desensitizing content.[3]

Dr. James Dobson's *Citizen* magazine reported on a police officer's view of how damaging such material can be for children:

San Jose, California, police officer Thomas C. Jensen, who investigates occult crimes and is considered an occult crime specialist, said he sees the result in children who are exposed to the kind of violence and fear portrayed in *Impressions*.

"This does affect children," he said. "I see how it affects them when they get older in criminal activity."

Jensen said *Impressions* contains rituals and symbols used in Wicca, a witchcraft religion; Satanism; and Santeria, a blend of the Aruba religion of Africa and [some rituals stolen from] Catholicism.

"By having the children sit in a circle and chant or prepare a spell that would send them somewhere or change them into something else, kids are participating in ritualistic activities in the classroom," Jensen said.[4]

## BEST-SELLER: THE SATANIC BIBLE

One result of such teaching is a growing acceptance of occult activity. We've known that the Satanists were out there ever since Anton LaVey established the First Church of Satan in San Francisco in 1966. We figured only a few fringe people took his *Satanic Bible* seriously. But now news reports tell us almost daily of frightening occult activity and satanic crimes on a large scale in our society, especially among youth.

According to Greg Reid, who leads a Christian youth group for teens coming out of Satanism—Anton LaVey has become a teen Satanist hero, and the *Satanic Bible* is a best-seller among teenagers. Why? Greg gives this answer:

Partly because it speaks to the pent-up anger and frustration of a lost generation... but I think there is a far deeper reason kids are being drawn to the deadly philosophy of the satanic church. They are spiritually empty. Yet, most teen Satanists have been raised in church! Somehow, their deepest needs for love, belonging, purpose and "overcoming power" have not been met. That need doesn't go away. Something must fill it.[5]

In his years of working with these teenagers, Greg has discovered how adult Satanists conduct carefully orchestrated recruitment programs aimed at young people.

## LOVE BOMBING

First, an adult Satanist who is designated to be a recruiter gets established as a respected member of a community through a business or profession. He or she often joins a church, makes large donations, and takes leadership positions in the congregation. The Satanist makes friends with a suitable recruit—a teen or young adult—and gradually introduces him or her to New Age philosophy. As the young person becomes fascinated with these new ideas, the recruiter progresses to seances, astral projection, and deeper forms of the occult. He also introduces the young person to a larger group of Satanists. Greg writes:

Animal sacrifice soon follows, and once the recruit is in too deep to get out, participation in human sacrifice is usually mandatory as a final initiation into Satanism. Once a blood oath is taken and signed, the recruit is ready to be sent out [as a recruiter himself].... He makes friends with kids who are angry, rebellious, lonely, and hurting. The leader is thoroughly trained in the Bible. To a teen recruiter, a weak Christian churchgoing kid is one of the highest prizes he can win for Satan, and it's very easy to confuse them quoting scriptures to destroy the doctrines they have only mentally accepted.[6]

The young leader will then throw a party (with no adults around) with lots of drugs, alcohol, and free sex. Ouija boards and other occult games are part of the entertainment. The leader looks for the youngster who shows a special interest in the games, and zeroes in. Greg continues:

The leader appears to be understanding (unlike parents), sympathetic, charismatic, fun-loving, and POWERFUL. There's an "aura" about him—scary but attractive.... He makes the recruit seem special. This is called "love bombing."

The recruit is invited to a second party.... There are less people. It is actually a "coven"... he is unaware that these are Satanists. The atmosphere [is] enhanced by candles, incense, and music—either Satanic metal or "new age" music. Other members are high on a variety of drugs. The high priest tells them about occult powers, how it helps them live strong and successful lives, free of outdated dead religion.[7]

A recruit who goes to the third party is invited to join the coven, which he usually does because of the gradual indoctrination, peer pressure, and the numbing effect of drugs. In the final step the recruit participates in a ritual in which an animal is killed, the recruit is given a chalice of blood to drink, and he signs an oath giving his soul to Satan.[8]

## WALK IN THE POWER OF GOD

It all seems too frightening to be real. But it is real, and it is happening to kids from Christian homes in our communities. We as "watchmen on the wall" need to be aware of Satan's devices and withstand his work through prayer and spiritual warfare. We truly are at war with Satan, and the lives of our children are at stake. Greg Reid declares:

To fight well you must walk in the power of God. No more ignoring the forces of evil. I challenge you with the words of one teen Satanist girl: "How do you expect me to believe your God has power over the devil if YOU don't believe it?"[9]

*Power* is the key word here. And power is what occultism is all about. An Arkansas pastor shared his experience in ministering to Kirby, a seventeen-year-old Satanist who came to him for deliverance at his parents' urging.

At age nine Kirby had gotten involved with a coven and was gradually trained in witchcraft without his parents' knowledge. He used his unusual psychic powers to manipulate people and get what he wanted, but at times the power frightened him. He was afraid he might harm someone.

His Christian parents worried about his rebellious behavior and his failing grades at school. The mother said that when she looked in his eyes, it was as if she was looking at a demon. After counseling with the pastor, the young man agreed to deliverance ministry. The pastor and a minister friend commanded the demons to leave, then led Kirby in a prayer of repentance and a prayer to renounce his occult activity.

For a period of time he was free. But in the end he was unwilling to turn his back on his power to manipulate people, and he would not give up having sex with his girlfriend. He chose demonic power and lust over God's plan for his life.

Earlier we discussed the effects of the sins and weaknesses of our forefathers. In Kirby's case, his maternal ancestors included witches, and he had exhibited a degree of psychic power from early childhood. The witches he became involved with recognized this tendency and seized upon it. Only by resolving to reject the works of evil in his life and willingly embrace God's ways will this young man be truly delivered.

## THE DANGER OF REBELLION

A primary problem many parents have with kids today is rebellion against any form of authority. In the story of Israel's King Saul we see that God considers this a serious sin. Through the prophet Samuel he said to Saul: "For rebellion is like the sin of divination, and arrogance like the evil of idolatry. Because you have rejected the word of the LORD, he has rejected you as king" (1 Sm 15:23, *NKJV*).

When teenage Robin rebelled and ran away from home, her mother, Jan, went to battle in her prayer closet.

Following are some of the Scripture prayers she prayed for Robin:

"Thank you, Lord, that you are able to save Robin, and that you will rescue her from the hand of the enemy (Dn 3:17).

"Father, I ask you to shine your light in Robin's heart, to give her the light of the knowledge of the glory of God in the face of Christ (2 Cor 4:6). Holy Spirit, turn Robin's heart to the Father, to walk in all his ways and to keep his commands (1 Kgs 8:58).

"I pray that Robin will be delivered from wicked and evil men. For the Lord is faithful, and he will strengthen and protect Robin from the evil one (2 Thes 3:2, 3).

"For this is what the Sovereign LORD says: I myself will search for my sheep and look after them.... I will search for the lost and bring back the strays. I will bind up the injured and strengthen the weak,... (Ez 34:11, 16)."

Jan also bound the lying spirits that would try to prevent Robin's heart from turning to the Lord. She asked God to place a hedge of protection around her as he did for Job (Job 1:10). She based other prayers on Jeremiah 1:12, Isaiah 55:11, Psalm 138:8, Zephaniah 3:7, and Jeremiah 24:7.

"When Robin returned home some days later with hair-raising stories of dangers she'd narrowly escaped, I realized how important my prayers and warfare had been," Jan concluded. "How I thank God for his faithfulness! Eventually she committed her life to the Lord."

## DEPRESSION, ANGER, SUICIDE

When Carrie's son Matt entered high school, he began having problems getting along with his father, who had grown up in a dysfunctional family. He continually criticized Matt, and he seemed incapable of showing him any affection or approval.

"I was constantly praying Malachi 4:6—that the heart of the father would be turned to his son and vice versa—and asking God to heal their relationship," Carrie says. "My husband got into therapy, but because of his own problem, he had difficulty trying to make things right with Matt.

"One day as I was in prayer the Lord said to me, 'Great fear is coming upon you, but you will have victory over it.' I didn't know what it was about, but I increased my prayer time, especially during our end-of-summer vacation. I was in deep intercession for our church and our pastor, as well as for my family."

When Matt began his senior year that fall he was depressed because he didn't like school, and upset that he didn't have a car of his own. Carrie was very concerned about his interest in Freddie Krueger, a character in a horror film, and was repelled by a poster Matt put up in his room with an alien monster figure on it.

"More than once I went into his room and bound the evil spirits I felt he was allowing into his life because of this interest. When I confronted him about the creature on the poster, he just laughed and said, 'He's my friend!'"

Shortly after school started, a tenth-grade boy in the community committed suicide by driving his car off a cliff. Matt's depression quickly got worse; once he told his father he felt his mind was about to snap. At times the oppression in the house was so heavy, Carrie would pray and praise and attack the enemy until it lifted. She and her husband prayed in agreement, pleading the blood of Jesus over Matt and asking God not to let their son commit suicide.

"One morning I had a heart-to-heart talk with Matt about his depression and his girlfriend problems, then shared some Scriptures with him before he left for school. Through the day I prayed, 'Lord, be a shield about him, be his glory and the lifter of his head' (Ps 3:3). I asked God to raise up intercessors to pray for my son. I sensed the need for much spiritual warfare on his behalf."

Late that afternoon Carrie returned from a brief shopping errand, just in time to see Matt as he was leaving for choir practice and Bible study.

"God bless you, Son," she said as he went out the door. "Have a good time, and I'll talk to you tonight." Carrie sensed this was a pronouncement somehow.

A few hours later Matt drove his mother's car off a three-hundred-foot cliff. It was the same area where the other boy had died, only higher up. Matt had said goodbye to his girlfriend, then drove to the cliff to read his Bible and pray, trying to reach God. Feeling there was no response, he started the car motor, rammed the accelerator, and drove off the cliff.

When the wheels left the road, Matt realized he had made a mistake. He prayed, "Jesus, please forgive me. Take me home." He really thought he was going to die. He blacked out just before the car landed.

A woman who lived nearby saw what happened and phoned the police as the car crashed on the rocky seashore below. Matt crawled from the wreckage in shock. Two Christian policemen walked up to him. "God must really love you, Son, because he saved your life," one of them said. These men had seen four or five other suicide attempts from that cliff; Matt is the only one who survived.

The policemen saw a Coast Guard helicopter overhead and signalled for help. "Who called you?" one of them yelled over the motor noise as they lifted Matt into the chopper.

"No one—I just happened to be in the area," the pilot answered.

Within minutes Matt was in the trauma unit of a nearby hospital. When his parents arrived, Matt was conscious and able to talk. What Carrie had spoken over her son that afternoon came true. God did bless him by saving his life, and she spoke to him *alive* that night!

Matt came through the experience miraculously. He had to wear a brace for a few months because of a back injury, and his parents put him in therapy with a Christian psychiatrist. The doctor couldn't understand what made Matt do this, as he said he had many patients from families with five times more problems who hadn't attempted anything so drastic. The Lord prompted Carrie to share with him something about the demonic realm.

In the emotional aftermath following the crash, Carrie cried out to God one day, "Oh, Lord, what was I doing at the exact moment of the crash?" He replied, "That makes no difference. What made a difference is what you were doing before the crash."

Matt continues to grow spiritually since the attack. He threw away his Freddie Krueger paraphernalia. While he was in the hospital, Carrie ripped the poster off the wall; Matt never objected. Carrie still prays for a deeper reconciliation between father and son, but she believes this battle is almost won!

## WHAT'S A MOTHER TO DO?

Be observant and aware of your children's activities, and try to meet their friends. It is important to pray that your children will form godly friendships; it's also good to pray for the friends themselves. Ask the Holy Spirit to show you specific areas you need to address in your prayers.[10]

Counselors working with youngsters who struggle with suicidal tendencies or get involved with the occult suggest being alert to these indicators:

- extreme mood swings: black depression, violent rage
- nightmares and deep fears
- withdrawal, rejection of family, noncommunication
- frequent absenteeism and lower grades in school
- interest in occult reading matter and horror movies
- secret friends and reluctance to have you meet them
- compulsive lying and excessive swearing
- rebellion
- interest in heavy-metal music
- sexual promiscuity.

If you suspect a child is now involved in or is being drawn toward these areas, your first recourse is naturally to pray. Pray for God's wisdom in handling the situation; also pray the child will have a revelation of truth and recognize the enemy's attempt to destroy him or her. It is helpful to pray in agreement with your husband or a prayer partner; don't carry the burden alone.

If you discover something questionable (such as a suicide note, occult objects, or drugs), ask the Lord to show you how and when to confront the child. Timing is important. Don't jump to conclusions or become angry. Give the child an opportunity to explain, and accept what he says at face value. Ask the Lord to reveal anything hidden; also ask him to show you whether the child should have professional Christian counseling.

## PERSISTENCE DEFEATED THE ENEMY

Here's how a friend of Quin's coped with her son's rebellion.

"Excuse me, Son," Hilda said, interrupting sixteen-year-old Jim as he shouted protests about his curfew hour while she cooked supper.

Pointing her finger toward the angry teenager, she said, "Satan, you can't have my son. I bind your activity in him, in the name of Jesus Christ."

"Now, Jim, what was that you were saying to me?" she asked calmly.

"Ohhhh Mom, I just forgot," he said and turned to leave the room.

It was the first time Hilda had used her authority as a believer in Jesus to come against the devil's manipulation or manifestation in one of her children. Though the four had been reared in a Christian environment, all of them rebelled and chose their own path instead of God's.

About the time Jim's rebellion became a problem, Hilda discovered through her Bible study that the fight was not with her son but with demonic forces that bound him. From that point on, her prayers intensified with one goal before her: to see Jim, still living at home, and all her other children turn to the Lord.

It was a long battle. Jim's rebellion persisted, leading him into drugs, crime, and a stint in jail. But for years this determined mother persisted in prayer and warfare. Jim was released from jail, got a job, and found a bride. But like his siblings, he continued to go his own way.

One year when all four of her adult children and their spouses were visiting for Christmas, Hilda told them the only gift she wanted from them was one hour of their attention. She set up her Sunday school flannelboard and took them on a Genesis-to-Revelation tour through the Bible, zeroing in on Christ's sacrifice on the cross for their sins. Captivated by her lesson, the young people sat around the dining table for two more hours asking Hilda questions.

The Holy Spirit began wooing them, and one by one over the next few months they all committed their lives to the Lord. Today all of them have a vital relationship with Jesus. They look back on that Christmas roundtable discussion as a turning point in their lives.

"The enemy had ensnared all my children, and I knew I had to fight for every one of them," Hilda explained. "It wasn't an easy battle. But knowing it was not God's will for any of them to perish, I persisted in telling Satan that they are God's property, and he had to take his hands off them!"

## "PRAY FOR YOUR CHILDREN" GROUPS

After reading Quin's book *How to Pray for Your Children*, and watching the accompanying video at a small retreat, five women in Kentucky had the idea of forming groups to pray for one another's children.

"Among the five of us we had about thirty children and grandchildren," Elizabeth, the leader, reported. "We saw the need to build a wall of prayer around these children, because the enemy obviously was seeking to destroy them. We spent time asking God to teach us how to pray and how to organize."

The women began to meet weekly in local parks and pray for one another's children. Then doors opened for them to share the vision in local churches, and they developed a format for groups within those churches.

The format is simple. Twenty or more women (sometimes husbands join them) meet for corporate prayer and sharing. They pray for one another's children in a general way, for the children of the community, and for the children of the nation. They also share testimonies of the results of prayer.

Then they break up into small groups of four or five. Each person in the small group shares a specific need about one of her children or grandchildren, then the group prays for that child. After praying together for the children individually by name, each woman takes the name of one child (other than her own) to pray for throughout the coming week. All needs shared in the small groups are held in confidence by those few people.

Every week the small groups are different. Sometimes the leader assigns people to groups as she is led by the Holy Spirit. Other times the larger group simply counts off to establish the small groups.

At a typical meeting parents gave the following "praise reports":

Mary had sent a tape series entitled "The Truth Will Set You Free" to her twenty-six-year-old daughter, a church dropout who was disillusioned about God. Mary had asked her small group to pray that Alice would listen to them. Two weeks later Alice called and said, "Thanks for the tapes, Mom. I've listened to six of them, and they're wonderful."

"It's a miracle that she listened to those tapes," Mary said. "I know the truth is setting her free!"

A couple shared their relief that twenty-two-year-old Carla had lost interest in a man who was twice her age. "We didn't do a lot of talking to her. We just prayed, and we asked our group to pray," they reported. "This man is very wealthy and offered a lot that could have turned her head. For a while she was seeing him almost every day. But through prayer the whole situation has been neutralized."

The original prayer group has multiplied—spreading into many churches in the Lexington area as praying parents unite to pray for one another's children.


WORD WARFARE

When twenty-year-old Anna dropped out of church and began devoting all her time to Barbara, a girl she'd met in college, Valerie, her adoptive mother, went to war using the Word of God. Anna had been disappointed by her boyfriend, then lost interest in men altogether. Valerie tried to talk to her about this unhealthy relationship, but Anna became very defensive and belligerent.

This praying mother recognized that Barbara was not the enemy, but only the means Satan was using to try to destroy

Anna and keep her from fulfilling God's call on her life. Valerie searched her Bible and compiled Scripture-based prayers which she prays for Anna daily. Some verses she paraphrased included these:

"Even the captives of the most mighty and most terrible shall all be freed; for he fights for those who fight with us and he saves our child, Anna (based on Is 49:25, *TLB*).

"Thank you, Lord, that you have hedged up Anna's way with thorns. You have built a wall against her, so that she cannot find her paths. She has followed after her lovers, but she shall not overtake them; Lord, you will betroth my daughter to you in stability and in faithfulness, and she will appreciate, give heed to, and cherish the Lord (based on Hos 2:6, 7, 19, *TAB*).

"The Sovereign Lord... wakes her ear to listen like one being taught.... She will not be rebellious, nor draw back from him (Is 50:4, 5).

"The Lord our God teaches Anna what is best for her; he directs her in the way she should go. She pays attention to his commands, her peace is like a river, her righteousness is like the waves of the sea (Is 48:17).

"The blood of Jesus purifies Anna from all sin... for he is the atoning sacrifice for her sins (1 Jn 1:7; 2:2)."

Valerie hasn't seen the turnaround she's asked God for, but she's standing in the gap for victory. One answer to prayer is that Anna sat down and shared her feelings with her mother, and she admitted some of the wrong attitudes she struggles with. She asked her mom to keep praying for her.

"The battle has been heavy," Valerie said, "but I'm staying very close to my Commanding Officer."

## Suggested Warfare Prayer for Children

"In the name and under the authority of Jesus Christ, my Lord, I bind all principalities, powers, and spiritual forces of evil in the heavenly realm exerting influence over my child[ren], _____ [name them]. Your assignments against them are cancelled by the blood of Jesus Christ.

"I bind and break spirits of witchcraft, occult activity, satanic interest, mind control, fantasy, lust, perversion, rebellion, rejection, suicide, anger, hatred, resentment, bitterness, unforgiveness, pride, deception, unbelief, fear, sensuality, greed, addictions, compulsive behavior [add others the Lord reveals]. I break their power and the power of rock music, and I declare them null and void in the lives of my children. The blinders the enemy has put on my children must go, in Jesus' name. My children *will* see the light of the gospel of Christ; they shall be taught of the Lord, and great will be their peace (Is 54:13).

"Father God, creator of all things, I thank you for the gift of my children. I ask you to dispatch angels to watch over them and protect them in all their ways (Ps 91:11). I ask you to send Christian friends into their lives to help them and be a godly influence. Lord, what an awesome privilege and responsibility to be a parent. Help me discern when my children need my prayers or my help. Give me wisdom to be the parent I need to be, and help me to be an understanding friend to them.

"Father, may my children fulfill your plan and purpose for their lives. May the Spirit of the Lord be upon them—the Spirit of wisdom and of understanding, the Spirit of counsel and of power, the Spirit of knowledge and of the fear of the Lord (Is 11:2). I release these gifts you've given me, Lord, and place my children in your hands. I thank you that you love them more than I do, that your plans for them are plans for welfare and peace, not for evil, and that you will give them a future of hope (Jer 29:11, *TAB*). Amen."

# TEN

# Fight for Your Marriage

*Wives, in the same way be submissive to your husbands so that, if any of them do not believe the word, they may be won over without words by the behavior of their wives, when they see the purity and reverence of your lives.*

**1 Peter 3:1-2**

"MY HUSBAND, a Bible study leader, is physically attracted to a woman in our church fellowship. Please pray with me for him, Ruthanne," Alicia pleaded after hearing me teach at a Canadian conference.

"When this woman goes to Carl's office for spiritual counsel, he puts everything aside to spend time with her. Yesterday he did it again," she continued, beginning to cry. "He didn't even bother to call and let me know he'd be late coming home. Sometimes I get so angry I just want to stop fighting for our marriage. He says he's not sexually involved with her, but he's playing with fire and doesn't even realize it. And he's an officer in the group sponsoring this conference!"

It's an all-too-familiar story of a Christian couple whose

marriage is under attack. Because of his pride and his carnal nature, the husband enjoys the interest and attention of a woman seeking his advice, yet he's blind to the danger involved. The wife recognizes the peril, but feeling hurt and rejected, she directs her anger at her husband instead of at Satan, the real enemy. The rift gets wider, and unless prayer and sober counsel prevail, divorce can result.

Reports of infidelity in Christian marriages have sent shock waves through the body of Christ in recent years. What is the answer? Is the influence of our permissive society just too great for Christians to overcome? What can a wife do under these circumstances?

I told Alicia that I felt Satan was using this woman's attention as a snare to ruin her husband's testimony and his marriage. I advised her to renounce her hurt and anger, then forgive both of them.

Alicia prayed and forgave Carl and the woman involved. Then we bound the spirits of deception, pride, and lust in both of them. We declared in the name of Jesus that all ties of sexual attraction between Carl and this woman, or any other women he had lusted after, were broken. We asked the Holy Spirit to reveal truth to him, to expose the enemy's snare, and to bring Carl to repentance.

"Now that you've released your husband from your judgment, the Holy Spirit is free to work in this situation," I told her. "Don't argue with him about it anymore. Just ask the Lord to help you express love to him."

I was astonished by the swift response to our prayer and spiritual warfare. After the meeting that same evening, I saw Alicia in the ladies' room, and she was radiant.

"Ruthanne, I can't believe the change in Carl!" she exclaimed. "The Lord must have dealt with him during the service, because he came down from the platform during the offering and apologized to me for his involvement with that woman and for hurting me. I told him I forgave him. His whole attitude has changed, and I know the Lord will help us work everything out."

This is an example of approaching a marital problem through spiritual warfare. And in this case it appears that a much more serious problem was avoided.


QUIN'S STORY


Marriages may be made in heaven, but they are lived out on earth with all our flaws exposed. We can choose either to allow hurts to ruin our marriage or to forgive and allow God to transform disappointments and wounds into a stronger relationship.

The way people hurt one another unwittingly can be painful beyond words. At least I have found it true.

I had never met any of my fiance's family until they came to Florida for our Christmas wedding. At the rehearsal dinner the night before the ceremony, LeRoy's dad announced to all my family, "Since LeRoy's been married before, this ceremony will be old hat to him."

I was devastated. Five years earlier LeRoy's first wife had died of leukemia. They had been married only two years. In my own vulnerability, nursing rejection since my parents' divorce when I was twelve, the message I perceived from my future father-in-law was not "Welcome to our family" but "You are second choice."

I cried all night and considered backing out of the marriage. Indeed, my courtship with LeRoy had been a two-year on-again, off-again relationship. I believed it had to do with his intermittently feeling unfaithful to his deceased wife. I felt I had to compete with her.

After we married I tried to forget the hurt, but then other wounding situations occurred. The first time we visited a new sister-in-law, she had all LeRoy's former in-laws waiting, and they greeted him with hugs and laughs. I slipped into the bathroom and had a long cry.

At his parents' house, pictures of "her" were displayed everywhere. She was a beautiful blonde, and I felt skinny and unattractive. Could I ever measure up?

I failed to communicate my hurt to LeRoy. He had married me, hadn't he? What was the big deal anyway? I repressed my feelings for years, not knowing how to get healed. Then one night I asked a pastor to pray for a fuller release of the Holy Spirit in my life. Before he would pray, he required me to forgive all who had wounded me.

I realized I not only needed to forgive my parents for the hurt and rejection I'd felt when they divorced, but I had to forgive my in-laws, who had unknowingly made me feel second-rate. And I needed to forgive LeRoy for not seeming to understand my feelings. I prayed a forgiveness prayer because the pastor asked me to do it, never realizing the impact or results I'd reap.

"Father, I forgive all who have hurt me: Daddy, Mom, Mama Sherrer, Pop Sherrer, LeRoy." I named others. "Now, Lord, forgive me for my anger, hurt, resentment, self-pity, and jealousy. I confess my sin. Thank you for your forgiveness. I receive it. Cleanse me and set me free."

It was the happiest event of my entire life. I felt a fresh outpouring of God's love, and LeRoy noticed the change. He said, "Honey, I wish this had happened a long time ago. You're better in every way. Whatever you've got, I want it!"

That was almost twenty years ago, and I've been married to my loving, gentle, wonderful husband more than thirty-five years now. Yes, like all couples we have misunderstandings to work through from time to time. But I know the solution is forgiveness and God's love.

## LOVE CAN BE TOUGH

In a recent marriage poll, *one hundred percent* of the women interviewed said they considered the most essential requirement for a spouse was faithfulness. Physical attraction was listed by only nineteen percent of the women (ages eighteen to twenty-four) as being essential.[1] Obviously, today's woman wants her husband to love her faithfully and exclusively all his days. Yet stark reality reveals that not all will.

Suppose your husband has had one affair after another and seems impervious to your efforts to get him to deal with the issue. What do you do?

"The lure of infidelity is an addiction to an individual who has a chink in his moral armor," says Dr. James Dobson, author of *Love Must Be Tough*. In discussing the cases of three wives he'd interviewed who put up with infidelity in their husbands without confronting them, he says:

While some people are chemically dependent on alcohol or heroin or cocaine, this kind of infidel is hooked on illicit sex. Psychologically, he needs the thrill of the chase, the clandestine meetings, the forbidden fruit, the flattery, the sexual conquest, the proof of manhood or womanhood, and in some cases, the discovery.

... What they needed were wives who were committed to the concept that *love must be tough.*

... What is required is a course of action—an ultimatum that demands a specific response and results in a consequence.[2]

A woman wrote Dr. Dobson telling of her experience after a counselor advised her to confront her adulterous husband, a pastor who had been dismissed from his church: "The counselor told me not to take the blame for my husband's affair, and that nothing I had done could justify his infidelity. He advised me to stand up and be firm with him, even though it would be difficult.

"A few months later the crisis came. I gave Milan an ultimatum: either go with the other woman or stay with me. He could not have both of us any longer. I put my hands on his shoulders and looked him straight in the eye and said, 'You know you are to blame for what has happened to us. You committed adultery, I didn't.' I told him if he loved the other woman more than me, then he should leave. I would accept it. I reminded him that he had a soul and would someday answer to God.

"Milan not only broke off the affair, but he later thanked me for having the courage to stick it out with him through this difficult time. It was not easy, but we worked it out and our family survived."[3]

## WHAT IS GOD'S STRATEGY?

A woman confronted with evidence that her husband is having an affair often goes to one of two extremes.

One is to ignore the evidence or rationalize it, and go on with life as if nothing has changed. Some men are happy to continue living two lives, and their wives accommodate them. In fact, in many parts of the world it is quite acceptable for a man to have a mistress on the side. Even worse, in some cultures a man is free to take a second wife and move her into the house. The first wife must either accept it or move out and support herself and her children. Ruthanne has counseled and prayed with scores of Christian women in Asia, Africa, and Latin America who face these situations.

The other reaction is to confront the husband prematurely out of hurt and anger. This kind of confrontation usually ends in an emotional shouting match, where nothing is resolved, but the breach is widened.

The wise woman who suspects her husband is unfaithful should first of all go to her prayer closet and seek God's direction. Recognize that your husband is not the enemy, nor is the "other woman." Satan is using human weaknesses to try to destroy your marriage. It is essential to have God's strategy in dealing with the situation.

Dr. Archibald Hart gives some further advice for a woman in this predicament:

> Divorce is not the only answer to an unhappy marriage. I am convinced that the solution to most miserable marriages is to be found in creative counseling, sound mar-

riage guidance, and, if necessary, individual therapy for the marriage partners—as well as in a mutual turning to God for help and healing.

... Of adults who are surveyed five years after their divorces, only about a quarter are resilient—managing to cope adequately with their new lives. Half are muddling along, just barely coping. And the final quarter are either failing to recover or looking back with intense longing to the time before their divorces, wishing the divorce had never taken place. Far from taking care of all their problems, for these people divorce has just added a whole set of new ones.[4]

## WHAT ABOUT INCEST?

When Sally's sixteen-year-old daughter told her that her father had been requiring sex of her since she was eight, Sally felt like she'd been hit with a sledgehammer. After twenty years of marriage, she realized her husband had been unfaithful right under their own roof. Not only did she hurt for her little girl, she had to face her own reactions.

"I went through the depths of despair, like someone with a mental illness. I wanted out of the marriage. I even considered starting a relationship with a single pastor I greatly admired because of his strong foundation in the Lord.

"As I prayed about my marriage, the Lord asked, 'Are you willing to be broken that this man may be healed?' I forgave him. From then on my commitment was set. In prayer I continually asked the Lord to give me understanding of my husband's feelings and problems. We got professional counseling and began to rebuild a marriage the enemy had tried to destroy.

"All this has been a slow process. But over a period of five years, trust has been reestablished and our relationship has been renewed. Our daughter has received counseling and healing. We've built a firm foundation with each other and our four children.

"I wouldn't want anyone else to go through this—but I know many women do. God was my strength through all the pain; without him I would not have made it."

## WHEN A MARRIAGE FAILS

Unfortunately, some marriages do fail. God does not force obedience; a spouse might choose the wrong path and leave the Christian wife or husband no recourse.

Even in this situation, God can bring his peace and strength if the Christian spouse looks to him. Dr. Hart advises immediate counseling for the newly divorced. He lists mistakes divorced people commonly make:

- condemning themselves, which intensifies their unhappiness
- not dealing with guilt feelings in a constructive way
- changing things too quickly, making adjustment even more difficult for all concerned
- making promises they can't keep
- forcing the children involved to make painful choices
- acting without a sense of self-awareness.[5]

Dane assured Lonnie he was a believer, but after the wedding she realized his deception. For eleven years she prayed for Dane's salvation. At times he went to church with her, but nothing in his life reflected a Christlike change.

Dane retired from the military, and they moved to the Middle East, where he worked for private industry and drew a huge salary. Consumed with greed, he stashed his money in Swiss bank accounts and invested in stocks and properties. These assets were placed in the names of various members of his family, but Lonnie found out much later that nothing was in her name.

While Dane's life was spinning out of control because of his alcoholism, Lonnie drew closer and closer to the Lord. Once after a six-day drunken binge, she heard what sounded like demons screaming through Dane's mouth, "Go in and kill her, go in and kill her, go in and kill her." She ran for her life.

Dane had been trained in psychological warfare, and he began using these tactics on Lonnie. He would tell lies about her, calling her a "spiritualist," and almost succeeded in turning her own parents and sons against her.

"I know God hates divorce, and I kept telling Dane I was committed to keeping our marriage together," she said. "But one day he filed divorce papers. Then I recognized that his heart was hardened not only against me but against God. And he denied he had an alcohol problem."

Lonnie learned that if a person will not yield his heart to the Lord, God will not overwhelm his will. Neither could she argue her husband into the kingdom. The divorce was granted, and Lonnie received only three years of alimony.

"I am confident the Lord will provide a meaningful life for

me," she said. "I had stood on the Word and declared Dane's salvation for so long, it became like an idol to me. I had to relinquish my husband to the Lord—totally release him. I believe someday, maybe when he hits bottom, he'll see his need for Jesus. In the meantime, I'm going on with God and trusting him to meet my needs."

## A WIFE LEARNS MERCY

In today's permissive society, pornography is a growing problem that threatens many Christian marriages. While Rachel's husband Bob was out-of-state for several months on a job assignment, she discovered that he had been making phone calls to pornographic 900 numbers and charging them on their charge cards. Rachel felt rejected, ugly, and cheapened. She called Bob and confronted him with what she had found out, flying into an emotional rage as she talked. He cried and said he wanted to come home and talk it over and work things out, but Rachel refused. As soon as she hung up, she called and scheduled an appointment with an attorney.

"Only then did I settle down and ask the Lord what he wanted me to do. He showed me that taking my case to a lawyer was not the answer. He told me to begin praying for a spirit of understanding. I cancelled the appointment and said, 'God, you told me you would be my defense—I'm depending upon you.'"

Later Rachel met one of Bob's aunts for the first time. From her she learned that Bob had suffered much rejection during his childhood. His mother had married five times while he was growing up, and he often went to this aunt's house to hide when he was afraid of being beaten by a stepfather.

Bob hadn't received affirmation or positive words as a child; now he was making these calls because he wanted to hear what he thought were "good things." Rachel realized that, if they get back together, she would need to speak positive words of life to him.

"As I was still struggling with my own hurt and rejection, God gave me a graphic illustration of the blessing of mercy. The year before I had opened a small business in my home, for which I filed sales tax receipts with the state each month. Now that the business had been dormant for six months, I assumed that I didn't need to send reports.

"One day a man from the state attorney's office came to my door and bluntly told me I could be prosecuted and sent to jail. Shaken, I explained that I simply was unaware that reports had to be filed if no sales were made, and my papers hadn't even been unpacked since our last move. Suddenly his gruff attitude changed. He said, 'Well, I'll have mercy on you this time. I'll take care of these reports for you.'

"After he left I stretched out on the sofa and cried. I was being bathed in mercy such as I had never experienced before, and I dropped off to sleep. When I woke up, I called Bob and told him I wanted to show him mercy. I was willing to talk things out."

The Lord gave Rachel Scriptures to pray for Bob: "Father, I pray that Bob will not set any vile thing before his eyes. . . . He will have nothing to do with evil (Ps 101:3, 4). Bob's body is not made for immorality, but for the Lord . . . (1 Cor 6:13). Thank you that he is free in Christ Jesus, and he will not be burdened again by a yoke of bondage (Gal 5:1)."

Many Scriptures also ministered to Rachel: "When anxiety was great within me, your consolation brought joy to my soul" (Ps 94:19). "When I called, you answered me; you made me bold and stouthearted" (Ps 138:3).

Bob came home, and the couple met with their pastor for counseling. Rachel asked Bob to forgive her for her bitter words, and the Lord helped her to begin speaking encouragement and life to him.

Rachel shares: "God not only set Bob free, but he did a lot of changing in me. For any woman facing this problem, I advise her to wait on the Lord before she takes any action. Then she should get counsel from a godly person and get her emotions under control before confronting her husband. We need to be willing to see the whole picture from God's point of view and work toward healing instead of rejection."

## WOMEN HAVE PROBLEMS TOO

Paul had a warning for the Christians in Ephesus: "But among you there must not be even a hint of sexual immorality, or of any kind of impurity, or of greed, because these are improper for God's holy people. Nor should there be obscenity, foolish talk or coarse joking, which are out of place, but rather thanksgiving. For of this you can be sure: No immoral, impure, or greedy person—such a man is an idolater—has any inheritance in the kingdom of Christ and of God" (Eph 5:3-5).

It's not always the men who get caught in the adultery trap, of course. We hear increasing reports of women who get involved with the boss at work, a trainer at the health spa, their pastor, or their best friend's husband. Of course, most of these women don't plan to have an affair. But they don't take precautions against it, and they fall into the trap.

"Beware of letting a male become your confidante," warns one woman who had a five-year affair with her married boss. She was devastated when he announced that he was taking a job in another city and that their relationship was finished. She turned to the Bible for comfort, recommitted her life to Christ, and set about saving her own marriage.

In her book *Feelings Women Rarely Share*, Judy Reamer offers her analysis:

> Some women... have become captive to their daydreams as a psychological haven from a world in which they can no longer cope.
>
> When a woman is not being emotionally satisfied in her marriage, she often begins to fantasize what another lifestyle may be like. Even though she may have a satisfying physical relationship with her husband, she still may feel deprived in the area of intimacy. She may be married to the strong, silent type who does not communicate or listen to what she is trying to say. Or she may be married to a selfish or demanding man who is a taker rather than a giver.... This woman begins to daydream what it would be like if only.... When unmet needs are combined with daydreams and fantasies, women become extremely vulnerable for an affair.
>
> ... Whether your source of sexual temptation is an old boyfriend, a man on the job, or only someone you have had a dream about, the solution is still the same... stop the

thoughts. Nip them in the bud... do not let your imagination run away with you.[6]

Judy goes on to suggest that if a woman is vulnerable to sexual temptation, she should refuse to even glance at the magazine racks in the grocery store, watch TV soap operas, review last night's passionate dream, or answer an old flame's letter or phone call. Her motto: "Affairs start in the head before they get to the bed."[7]

Putting on our gospel armor and meditating on the Word of God—a weapon sharper than any two-edged sword—helps us get out and stay out of immoral relationships.

## Prayer for a Believing Husband

"Lord, thank you for the marriage partner you have blessed me with. Show me how to love him with your love—to revere and honor and trust him all the days of his life. Help me to speak with wisdom, but always with the law of kindness on my tongue (Prv 31:26). May my husband love me as Christ loved the church, and together may we serve you.

"Lord, give us both a spirit of wisdom and revelation, so that we may know you better (Eph 1:17), and give us a deeper understanding of your Word as we seek to live by its guidance.

"Give him direction for our family. May he increase in wisdom and favor with you and his working associates, and reach his full potential as a man of God. Provide for his emotional, physical, and spiritual needs. Protect him from the fiery darts of the evil one. Help him to be the father and grandfather you intended for him to be, a godly influence and a blessing to all who know him. Amen."

## Prayer for an Unbelieving Husband

"Lord, my husband doesn't know you, and it grieves me so. I know you love him, and that Jesus came and died to save the lost. Open my husband's eyes that he may see the Truth, which is Jesus. I pray he will see Jesus in my life. Help me to see him with your eyes and love him with your love.

"In the name of Jesus I bind all evil spirits that are keeping him from knowing his heavenly Father. Lord, I pray you will send a godly man to share the gospel with him in a way he can understand and receive.

"Father, grant him repentance leading to the knowledge of the truth, that he may come to his senses and escape from the snare of the devil, having been held captive by him to do his will. Lord, open his eyes so that he can turn from darkness to light and from the dominion of Satan to your kingdom, in order that he may receive forgiveness of sins and an inheritance among those who have been sanctified by faith in you (based on 2 Tm 2:25b, 26; Acts 26:18, *NAS*). Thank you, Lord, for working in his life until this prayer is answered. In Jesus' name. Amen."

# ELEVEN

# Spiritual Healing and Warfare

*He [Jesus] called his twelve disciples to him and gave them authority to drive out evil spirits and to heal every disease and sickness.* **Matthew 10:1**

NORM WAS SITTING in church one Sunday night when suddenly he tried to speak and couldn't. His wife Jean drove him to the hospital, and after tests, the neurologist diagnosed encephalitis.

He explained that the effect of the infection was to cause small "blisters" to form on Norm's brain. He could die by morning. Jean gave approval for an experimental treatment. The doctors could not guarantee there would be no adverse side effects.

"I know the enemy was out to kill him," Jean says. "We learned he'd been bitten by a mosquito that had bitten a horse infected with encephalitis. It was as if a thief had crept up on Norm in the form of a little mosquito. I was indignant. I said, 'Devil, how dare you do this! You'll not have my husband. God's not finished with him.'"

For twelve days Norm fought for life, sometimes so delirious with pain that his wife and a friend had to hold him on the bed, even though he was in arm restraints. A prayer alert went out: *Norm's in trouble.* Prayer groups all over Texas joined in intercession and warfare for his recovery. Many came to the hospital to keep prayer vigils.

On the thirteenth day the crisis was over. He recuperated at home for two more weeks, then returned to his job as a pharmacist, with no side effects of the disease or the medication. The doctor told Jean he'd not known anyone to survive what Norm had gone through.

While she is grateful for the medical help, Jean believes prayer and spiritual warfare were essential. "I felt my job was to stand in the gap and keep breaking that deadly germ's hold on Norm," she says.


## HEALING: NOT A FORMULA

Three outstanding healings that Jesus performed are recorded in the fifth chapter of Mark.

There is a man so tormented by evil spirits that he has supernatural strength. When he encounters Jesus, he falls at his feet. Jesus commands the evil spirits to come out of him and go into a herd of pigs. Immediately the man is restored to his right mind.

Next is the account of a woman who has been bleeding for twelve years but has gotten no help from doctors. Pressing through the crowds around Jesus, she reaches out and touches his cloak. Immediately her bleeding stops. "Daughter, your faith has healed you. Go in peace and be freed from your suffering," Jesus tells her.

On the way to Jairus' house to heal his daughter, Jesus hears that she is dead. With the child's mother and father and his own disciples, Jesus enters the room. Taking her by the hand he commands, "Little girl, I say to you, get up." The twelve-year-old stands up, walks around, and eats a meal. Not just healed, but brought back to life.

There is no one-two-three formula for healing, any more than there is a formula for spiritual warfare. Sometimes healing comes through casting out demonic spirits, sometimes by the faith of the person who is ill, sometimes by a prayer of agreement—but always by Jesus' sovereign supernatural touch.

We read about healing miracles in the early church, when the sick were laid in the streets so that Peter's shadow could fall on them: "Crowds gathered from the towns around Jerusalem, bringing their sick and those tormented by evil spirits, and all of them were healed" (Acts 5:16). Notice that *all* were healed—those with evil spirits and those with physical infirmities.

God's power to heal certainly has not diminished today. Sometimes he uses doctors and modern medical technology, as well as prayer and spiritual warfare, to bring about healing. Ruthanne interviewed a surgeon in her city who used to be outraged when he saw ministers praying for the sick.

"I felt they were infringing on my territory," he said. "I figured they should stick to preaching and let me and my professional colleagues in medicine take care of the sick. But then I became aware of the work of the Holy Spirit. A while later Kathryn Kuhlman had a meeting in our city. I was invited to sit on the platform. A woman who was bent over, crippled by disease and in constant pain, was healed before my eyes. I heard her bones snap as she stood up straight and began to walk freely, praising God.

"After that I began praying for my patients, and I realized I needed God's partnership in trying to help them."

## HEALING SCRIPTURES

When Jamie Buckingham, well-known author and pastor of a Florida congregation, learned he had cancer, he took his wife Jackie into the den to give her the doctor's diagnosis: "Renal cell carcinoma—cancer of the kidney. It has spread to the lymph glands and appears inoperable. Prognosis is poor."

Jackie remembers that day clearly. "I said to Jamie, 'I'm not going to receive this. We'll get the best help we can. You aren't going to die and leave me!' Something just rose up in me to fight it."

Jamie admitted to Jackie how Satan was assailing his mind with accusations such as, "You are filled with sin, you judge God's people, you don't love your wife, you're proud. You will die."

Her response was immediate. "I told Jamie we would repent together until we were assured that all corruption was gone. Jesus died at Calvary for our sins and our diseases, so we can enjoy his presence with a clean and pure heart."

Faith rose up like a geyser in Jackie as she blurted out, "God has told me this is not unto death. We may go through the fire, but we shall emerge on the other side, Jamie."

Jackie wrote healing verses on yellow sheets of paper and

plastered them all over their two-story house—on bedroom walls, bathroom mirrors, the refrigerator door. Everywhere they looked they saw God's promises.

"Lord, give us directions—for the right doctors, the right decisions, for a group of intercessors," they prayed. People in their church began praying during specific time-slots. Early on when they asked what they could do, the Buckinghams replied, "Pray that we can sleep!"

"Others prayed, and we slept," Jackie told Quin. "Sometimes while Jamie slept, I'd lay hands on him and pray Scriptures over him. Once I made the sign of the cross on his back as I prayed for his healing, referring back to Calvary where it all began. If Jesus died for our sickness, it was done. We just had to appropriate it.

"While we slept we played tapes of healing Scriptures, as well as praise and worship tapes. When we were in a car, I'd read Scriptures aloud.

"Hold fast the profession of your faith, Jamie, without wavering, for he who promised is faithful (Heb 10:23, *KJV*).

"Jamie, Jesus took up your infirmities,... was crushed for your iniquities,... and by his wounds you are healed (Is 53:4, 5).

"Jamie, God says, 'My son,... listen closely to my words;... keep them within your heart, for they are life... and health to your whole body' (Prv 4:20, 22)."

## I SHALL NOT DIE, BUT LIVE!

"We determined that our minds would be stayed on God and his promises," Jackie shared with Quin in a phone visit.

"God gave me a special gift of faith that we'd come through it—we *would* come out victorious. But I felt the Lord told me I was to keep building up Jamie's faith."

Together they determined to stake their lives on God's Word, believing this key Scripture for Jamie: "I shall not die, but live, and declare the works of the Lord" (Ps 118:17, *NKJV*).

"Our family and church went into deep intercession, and we heard from many around the world who were praying for Jamie too," Jackie says.

Through a series of Spirit-led incidents and "divine appointments," Jamie decided to risk surgery rather than having treatment. It was a difficult decision because he'd been told initially that surgery could be life-threatening.

As Jamie was being prepared for surgery in a Houston hospital, Jackie, their daughter, a sister, and a few close friends gathered about his bed to commit him to the Lord. They asked God to give the surgeons wisdom and to station angels in the operating room.

The surgeon removed a kidney and a huge growth in his renal vein, as well as numerous lymph nodes. After seven hours of surgery the doctors said, "We got it all." A week later when all test results were in, Jamie learned the lymph glands were free of cancer. The disease had been limited to the kidney, and no further treatment was necessary.

"What a time of rejoicing we had! Jamie would not die but live and declare the works of the Lord," Jackie told me.

But later, while Jamie was still recovering at home, the enemy hit him again, this time with depression.

Jamie remembers:

Even after going back to my surgeon ten weeks following the operation and undergoing extensive tests which proved I was indeed healed, Satan kept trying to pull me down. "Nobody escapes cancer. You may have squeezed through this time, but I'll be back with seven worse devils."

"... Depression, like an evening fog, would settle in—obliterating all God had done, hiding his wonderful promises. I never caved in. But it was often there, especially when I heard reports of others—some dear friends—who were dying or had died of the same thing God had delivered me from.

"Help for the depression came from... the prayers of my wife and close friends, who sensed when the fog was settling and entered into spiritual warfare on my behalf. In those times—and they seldom lasted longer than a few minutes—my wife would start a barrage against Satan with the Word of God. He *always* fled when hit with that kind of artillery.[1]

Jamie has since been through two more minor bouts with cancer in his spine and lung which were sucessfully treated with radiation. Jackie's faith and encouragement, coupled with the prayer support of family, friends, and even strangers, helped bring Jamie through to victory during each crisis.

## CHOOSE LIFE!

Fran is a contemporary daughter of faith who learned a new depth of spiritual warfare when her husband needed emergency heart surgery. Mike had been in a wheelchair for thirty-five years as a result of polio. He was now a sixty-seven-year-old triplegic with heart complications. Doctors said that his chances of survival were extremely slim.

Just before he was air-evacuated to a large city medical center, a prayer partner called to give Fran a Scripture verse to encourage Mike: "When I passed by you and saw you squirming in your blood, I said to you while you were in your blood, 'Live!'" (Ez 16:6, *NAS*).

The night before surgery Fran had a serious talk with her husband. "Mike, do you want to live?" she asked him. "I don't want you to be praying to die, while I'm praying for you to live. I want to honor what you want, because I know things could get very rough."

"I want to live, Fran," he assured her. "I feel God has some things left for me to do with my life. I love life, so of course I want to live."

Fran held Mike's hand and prayed aloud: "Lord, we come in a prayer of agreement to say *Mike chooses life.* If we hit any tight places in the days ahead, we are in agreement with your word to Mike that he does choose life. Thank you, Lord."

The surgery was normal with no complications. When the doctors felt all was under control, they allowed Mike to make the six-hour trip back to his home. But that first night home he began to hemorrhage.

An ambulance rushed him to the local hospital, where his condition was stabilized with blood transfusions. Over the next forty days he literally fought for his life, as fifteen more units of blood were pumped into him.

One night when he was out of the intensive care unit and back in a private hospital room, he began to hemorrhage once again. Fran was alone with him. She ran to the nurses' station for help. Soon a medical team was scurrying, getting I.V.s going in his arms, legs, and chest. His vascular system was collapsing. There was no detectable blood pressure. Fran, a nurse, knew Mike was dying.

While the hospital team was working, she knelt down and looked Mike in the eye. Though he couldn't respond, she knew he could hear her.

"Mike, choose life," she shouted. "Choose life, Mike. Choose life… choose life… choose life. You will not die, but live. Choose life."

Fran watched Mike's eyes until she was sure he understood. Even though he still couldn't breathe on his own, she knew that both fight and light had come back into him.

During his long hospital stay, prayer warriors gathered outside his hospital room day and night to join Fran in fighting for Mike's life. They'd pray, saying Bible verses aloud, then declare to the devil that he wasn't going to snuff out Mike's life until it was God's exact timing for him to go to heaven. He would live.

And live he did. For the past three years Mike has been active again in his wheelchair.

## BATTLE OF THE MIND

More than eighteen years ago Arlene was in the final, hopeless stages of multiple sclerosis. One night she had a dream in which she saw an open grave. She knew it was hers, and fear squeezed her into the darkness. Then she heard a voice say, "Don't look down. Look up!" She awoke mystified and asked the Lord what the dream meant.

In her spirit she heard his reply: "Arlene, don't focus on the circumstances. Don't look at your problem. Look at me. Look at my resources. Look at my love. Don't look down. Look up!"

Arlene learned the futility of calling detente with Satan. We can't say to him, "You leave me alone; I'll leave you alone."

"When we don't see a way out, our hearts falter and we find ourselves right where the devil wants us," she explains. "He sucks us into the mire of helplessness and a 'no win' situation."

After the Lord gave her that dream, Arlene began to believe God to do the impossible. She resisted the oppression of the enemy against her mind, and declared the truth of God's Word. Just as Nehemiah saw victory by refusing to go to the Plain of Ono to talk with the enemy who was taunting him (Neh 6:2, 3), Arlene also experienced victory as she followed the Lord's instructions to her. She filled her thoughts with God's Word and resisted Satan's attack against her mind. Later she attended a healing service, where God healed her instantly.

Here's the principle God taught her that night about his divine perspective. Notice the contrast:

| In the Spirit | In the Natural |
|---|---|
| Seated in heavenly places | In the Plain of "Oh no!" |
| Alert and active | Drowsy and inactive |
| Beholding him | Focusing on our problem |

| In the Spirit | In the Natural |
|---|---|
| Moving in divine revelation | Listening to Satan's mockery |
| Receiving the kingdom | Calling "detente" |
| Confident of victory | Defeated |

Arlene says, "God is calling his warriors to battle. Everything Jesus used to defeat Satan is available to us. When Jesus prayed, he looked up. When the enemy tried to flood his mind, Jesus 'listened upward' and spoke the Word of God to defeat Satan. His mind was a storehouse of the words of God.

"No matter how defeated you may have felt in the past, no matter how your mind has been assailed by the enemy, change your mind to agree with God's best. Recognize that we have the mind of Christ (1 Cor 2:16), and look up to see his triumph."[2]

## DIVINE BLOOD SUPPLY

When Paula's granddaughter Tiffany was three days old, she had a seizure. The doctor in intensive care told the family, "The right front side of the brain is destroyed."

But Paula and Jim, as grandparents, began a barrage of prayer using the Word of God to come against Satan's plan to kill or cripple Tiffany. Jim would declare, "Satan, you have no legal right to attack this baby. She's bone of my bone and flesh of my flesh."

The Holy Spirit prompted Jim to pray about the blood

supply to the baby's brain. "God, put a new blood supply to the part of her brain that is damaged. I thank you for hearing me. I thank you for doing it. New blood supply to her brain, Lord, new blood supply. Thank you, Lord."

Finally Jim and Paula felt peaceful and stopped their warring. A nurse later came to tell them the baby had stopped having seizures. When Jim asked what time the seizures had stopped, he learned it was the exact moment he'd felt it was time to stop battling.

Four days later Tiffany went home from the hospital and never had another symptom. When her parents took her for her six-month check-up, the doctors said new blood had gone to the part of her brain that had been damaged, just as Jim had prayed. Today she is healthy and above normal in her development.

## PRAYING AROUND THE CLOCK

Having been born with a kidney disease, most of Jody's young life had been plagued with illness. By the time he was eight years old, treatment with a dialysis machine was no longer effective.

Finally Jody received a kidney transplant from his father. All went well until the third day, when the transplanted kidney stopped functioning. The doctor told his mother, Sharon, that the kidney would have to be removed the next day.

"No, wait. I have a church family who prays," she begged.

Sharon called Barbara, the pastor's wife, who called two other prayer warriors to join her immediately. That night at the midweek service, volunteers signed up to take one-hour shifts around the clock to pray that Jody's body would not reject the new kidney.

"We are to pray until he comes home from the hospital," Barbara instructed the volunteers. "No letting up. Jody's life depends on this prayer, so please don't sign up unless you intend to keep your commitment."

Prayer warriors filled all the time-slots and went to battle. Within twenty-four hours the kidney began functioning properly, but the prayer support team kept praying until Jody left the hospital. Amazingly, he was able to leave the hospital on the day originally scheduled for his dismissal, before the rejection problem had developed.

Later, when Barbara visited him at home, he told her that whenever he was in a lot of pain at the hospital, there was something like a dark cloud that would hover over his bed. But when his mother or grandmother prayed, it would disappear through the wall. When they stopped praying, that "something" returned to hover over his bed, and he would again have extreme pain. The prayers literally drove away the spirits of death, pain, and oppression that tried to take the child's life.

Now, five years later, Jody's transplanted kidney continues to function normally.


## SATAN'S COUNTERFEIT

God's best is for us to walk in divine health, although many complex factors—some of them our fault, some of them the work of the enemy—frustrate God's highest plan for our lives. But one thing is clear in Scripture. The devil's intent is always to "steal and kill and destroy" (Jn 10:10).

We've already discussed the increase of occult activity and a growing acceptance of New Age philosophy in our society. The practice of "white witchcraft"—supposedly done for good and unselfish purposes—is a part of this trend. But we must never forget that if the devil does anything, even something that appears to be good, we must consider the source and reject it as evil.

John warns us: "Dear friends, do not believe every spirit, but test the spirits to see whether they are from God, because many false prophets have gone out into the world. This is how you can recognize the Spirit of God: Every spirit that acknowledges that Jesus Christ has come in the flesh is from God, but every spirit that does not acknowledge Jesus is not from God. This is the spirit of the antichrist, which you have heard is coming and even now is already in the world" (1 Jn 4:1-3).

Johanna Michaelsen, who before her conversion was involved with a psychic practitioner, writes:

After almost two centuries of general skepticism toward the "miraculous," the secular world is being bombarded with growing evidence that there are indeed forces beyond the scope of the normal scientific process.

... There is definite, validated evidence that unexplainable phenomena are taking place in various occult practices. Medical doctors have verified many incidences of supernatural physical cures performed by psychic surgeons.[3]

I have seen many people miraculously healed by the Hand of God through prayer, including my own husband, who was healed overnight when God literally fused together two painful disintegrating vertebrae.... *The original does exist.* That is precisely why Satan is busy producing counterfeits to the work of God through psychics and mediums. That is to be expected of him.... We shouldn't be too surprised to find practicing occultists within most of our denominations.[4]

... As believers our call is to focus on Jesus, to worship *Him,* to keep our eyes on *Him,* to come to know and love and experience Him above all else.[5]

In every situation we face where spiritual warfare is called for, we need God's direction for wisdom and discernment. Let us not be deceived by Satan's counterfeit.

WHEN HEALING DOESN'T COME

While the examples of healing we've shared are primarily victories, it is realistic to recognize that there is a time when we all die. However, I don't believe it is God's best that we die due to disease.

Quin's Mom, after thirteen months of fighting cancer, supported with lots of prayer and good medical treatment, died. During her illness Jewett meditated on numerous healing Scriptures as well as those about heaven. Three weeks before her death, while in a semi-comatose state, having spoken no words in days, right after I read her a Bible passage and prayed the Lord's prayer, she rose up in bed and shouted, "Hallelujah, Hallelujah, Hallelujah!" It was my best birthday present ever and her last words on earth.

As her primary caregiver, I was relieved when she finally slipped into heaven, no longer to suffer. Two days after her funeral, my husband as layreader stood in the pulpit to read a passage selected for every church in our denomination for that Sunday. Knowing my mom was now with Jesus, this verse he read had special significance. *"My ears had heard of you, but now my eyes have seen you"* (Job 42:5).

Do I still believe in healing? Absolutely yes! I've prayed for people to be healed since and have seen God touch them with his healing virtue. Halfway through writing this book, my husband LeRoy was hospitalized with severe hip pain, and all tests showed a "hot spot" highly suspicious of cancer. After a bombardment of prayer by many Christians, and God's mercy, he was healed within two weeks, to the astonishment of his medical specialists.

From my study of the Bible, I continue to believe it is my business to pray and God's business to heal, in his way and his timing. He still gives his disciples authority to drive out evil spirits and heal sickness, in his mighty name.

Let's not stop.

# TWELVE

# How Can I Tell If I'm under Attack?

*Beloved, do not think it strange concerning the fiery trial which is to try you, as though some strange thing happened to you; but rejoice to the extent that you partake of Christ's sufferings.* **1 Peter 4:12, 13, NKJV**

By now you've discovered that just because you are a Christian, you are not immune to the attacks of the evil one. But you have a direct line to the One who can free and heal. How do you know if you are under attack? How can you discern whether evil forces are at work in your life or if it's God at work?

Quin once heard a teacher suggest that you ask yourself: Is what I'm experiencing a temptation, a test, or an attack?

If it's a temptation, I want to resist! I could choose to say as Joseph did when tempted by Potiphar's wife, "How then could I do such a wicked thing and sin against God?" (Gn 39:9).

If it's a test sent by the Lord to teach me something, I want to learn. But if it's an attack from Satan, I want to fight.

Does God test us and teach us? Yes. We read of his dealings with Israel: "These are the nations the LORD left to test all those Israelites who had not experienced any of the wars in Canaan (he did this only to teach warfare to the descendants of the Israelites who had not had previous battle experience)... " (Jgs 3:1-2).

God wanted the younger Israelites to learn war. We need to ask God what it is he wants us to learn in the situation we're going through, and trust him to show us.

WHAT IS THIS, LORD?

JoAnne, an intercessor for a major Christian ministry, awoke one morning feeling as if she'd been kicked in the head by a horse. In moments she was partially paralyzed. Rousing her sleeping husband, a military doctor, she told him, "You'd better get me to the hospital; I can't move!"

While waiting for the ambulance, JoAnne began praying, "Lord, are you about to take me home? If you are, I'm ready. But if this is an attack from Satan, I need to know so I can fight. Which is it?"

"An attack!" She felt she'd clearly heard God's word.

"Lord, I know what to do with an attack—fight. And I'll fight for all I'm worth, because that means you have something greater in mind for me. Now, please enable me to fight."

"Stand. I'm in this with you," the Lord seemed to assure her.

During the next few days in the hospital, whenever she'd feel another swift "kick in the head" she'd say, "Satan, you've come far enough. You can't kill me. I'm hidden in Jesus. By his stripes I am healed. Now back off." Then she'd sing and worship God for a long time.

The doctors ran numerous tests and even sent her to an out-of-state hospital. They never definitely diagnosed her illness, but found that an artery in her head was smaller than normal, possibly a condition she'd had since birth. One doctor told her plainly, "I do not know what's wrong." Finally the paralysis and excruciating headaches left her, and she went back to her usual routine.

But whenever JoAnne feels another swift blow to her head, she knows it's an attack from Satan. She tells him, "Devil, and every demon spirit coming against my body to give me this infirmity, I tell you to stop your maneuvers in the name of my Savior, Jesus Christ. You are a defeated foe, and I am redeemed by the blood of Jesus."

## DOING SOMETHING WRONG?

Ruthanne was teaching on spiritual warfare for a women's group in East Texas. Afterward a woman shared that in her two-year Christian walk, she had led several family members to accept the Lord also. But she was troubled about serious problems now facing her.

"Am I doing something wrong?" she asked.

"No, it's not that you're doing anything wrong. Your praying and witnessing have made you a prime target for the enemy," I assured her. "Actually, you should be encouraged to know you are a threat to the devil's kingdom. Take up your weapons and fight!"

Helping her with guidelines to go along with the lesson I'd just taught, I prayed with her and encouraged her to find a prayer partner to stand with her in warfare concerning her family problems.

Her question—"Am I doing something wrong?"—is one all of us ask at one time or another. How do we tell whether we're off the track somewhere or under enemy attack? Is the enemy opposing me, or is God trying to tell me something?

"When the enemy attacks, there is great condemnation and seemingly no way out," a pastor's wife told me. "I distinguish by recognizing the difference between condemnation and conviction. Condemnation brings hopelessness. When the Holy Spirit convicts, there is a way out. I can confess my sin—of gossip, lying, or whatever—and receive forgiveness and cleansing."

"The enemy will try to defeat us in some area, or even remove us from the spiritual race entirely," another friend said. "God's correction, on the other hand, exposes a heart condition or weakness in some area. God's correction gets us a better place in the race and keeps us in focus."

"I have contested and rebelled against God's roadblocks," a young graduate student told me. "But I knew that I was acting in defiance of God rather than against the crippling influence of evil. Attacks by evil forces generally have been accompanied by a spiritual prompting for prayer against the opposition."

Here we contrast the characteristics of these two types of trial:

| Enemy Attack | God's Correction |
|---|---|
| accusation, condemnation of *you* | conviction concerning the *attitude* or *deed* |
| depression | call to repentance |
| hopelessness | assurance of forgiveness |
| destruction of self-esteem | restoration of a sense of value as God's child |

## FACTORS THAT GIVE THE ENEMY ACCESS

We asked more than a hundred intercessors, "What makes a believer vulnerable to the enemy's attack?" They mentioned these major ways we could give the enemy access to our hearts, minds, and bodies:

- sin: immoral behavior, disobedience, anger, pride, rebellion, unforgiveness, criticism, selfishness, and so on
- ignorance of Satan's devices and characteristics
- compromise with the enemy
- limited knowledge of God's Word and his purposes
- not spending time with the Lord (lack of discipline and vigilance; becoming careless or passive)
- lack of focus or persistence
- failure to use spiritual weapons (due to the above reasons)
- getting our eyes off Jesus and onto our problems
- immaturity: "blind spots" or areas of our life not yielded to the lordship of Jesus
- fatigue—physical, emotional, or spiritual

- preoccupation with self and physical comfort
- inadequate prayer from others
- disunity with fellow Christians and in the home.

## REPEATED ATTACK

Sometimes, however, there seems to be no chink in your armor, no disobedience to God, no willful sinning, when *pow,* here comes an arrow—aimed at putting you out of existence. Rowena felt like that when a drunk driver hit her car, causing serious injuries. God showed her that the accident was definitely an arrow from the bow of the enemy.

Since the Bible says, "No weapon forged against you shall prevail" (Is 54:17), Rowena claimed that verse as she began her long convalescence. She also meditated on Psalm 23:4: "though I walk through the valley of the shadow of death, I will fear no evil." When doctors said she might never walk again, she clung to that Scripture and used it in warfare. And she did walk again.

Five years later she had another car wreck. She was able to get out of the car and run to safety, just before her car rolled over an embankment and was totalled.

"This time a righteous indignation arose in me," she said. "I found that once again I had to put a guard on my mind by quoting Scriptures to resist fear that my life might be totally destroyed. Only a renewed mind can rise up in times of attack and defeat the purposes of the enemy."

## WHOSE VOICE IS THAT?

Women have often shared with us experiences of "hearing a voice" and wondering whether it was from God or not. Actually, there are three possibilities:

1. It could be God speaking through the Holy Spirit. In this case, whatever is spoken will be consistent with God's character and his Word.
2. It could be a demonic voice representing Satan.
3. It could be your own inner voice "speaking" a thought based on your logical reasoning, your will, or your self-centered emotions.

If you have difficulty discerning which it might be, you may want to pray: "Lord, I desire to hear your voice and be led by you. If this is your Holy Spirit speaking, please cause this impression I have to become clearer and more urgent. If you want me to take any action, cause the urge to do this thing to *increase*. If this impression I have is *not* of you, please cause it to fade.

"By the authority of the blood of Jesus which covers me, I address any evil spirits present and command them to be silent, in Jesus' name, and to flee. I silence the voice of my own reasoning, desires, and feelings. I refuse to hear any alien voice; I will listen only to the voice of my Shepherd.

"Thank you, Father, for speaking to me by whatever means you choose as I wait upon you. I promise to obey that which you speak."

## ENEMY VOICE

When the hospital nurse brought Ruby's newborn to her for the first time, she was repulsed by the sight of her four-and-a-half pound preemie. He looked like an ugly, shriveled-up, ninety-year-old man. In her mind she heard a voice say, "Throw him on the floor. You don't want him. Throw him on the floor."

"I hugged him to my bosom and withdrew into a corner of the room as though to protect us both," Ruby recalled. "Since I had lost three babies through miscarriages, I had bargained with God for this baby, as Hannah did for her son Samuel. Naming him Michael, for the warrior angel, I promised God he would be a mighty warrior for him."

Ruby recognized that an enemy voice had told her to destroy her baby, and she refused to take heed. "It was as real as any voice I've ever heard," she said. "I know God gives life; he doesn't destroy. So I had no trouble knowing this was not God but an attack from Satan himself, and I ordered him to leave."

## HEAD-ON ENCOUNTER

A woman who had a head-on encounter with demons shares her story:

"I had a degree in philosophy and religion, and in my search for reality I had experimented with drugs. I was lonely, empty, unhappy, restless, unfulfilled, and definitely godless. I had a little money to spare, so I was the drug pusher's dream. I attracted some pretty rough characters who wanted to dominate my days and nights.

"Friends told me about the Lord. I could not relate, but seeds were planted. One friend brought me a Bible. I laughed her all the way out the door, but I kept the Bible. One night when I was very lonely, I began reading it and realized this was truth. I accepted the Lord and felt the 'rushing wind' of the Holy Spirit encompass me in my room that night.

"But the very next day I began to see and hear evil spirits. Although I was uneducated in the things of the Lord, I felt as though there was a massive spiritual war going on around me. Was I going mad? Were the drugs I had taken causing me to hallucinate? I asked my father to take me to the hospital, because I was still seeing and hearing evil spirits.

"On the sixth floor of the hospital, one of the evil spirits spoke directly to me and said 'they' were going to get me for sure this time. I knew nothing of how to resist the devil, and I was terrified. Not realizing how far up in the air I was (about a hundred feet), I jumped out the window, calling on the Lord to help me.

"I was broken in pieces—my back splintered, both legs and feet crushed, and my lungs punctured by broken ribs. Nevertheless, my head was intact and my spinal cord untouched. The evil spirits disappeared. The Lord definitely cared for me in the ensuing days and months.

"After two months I was in rehabilitation and walking again. After five months my back braces and casts were removed. About a year later the Lord began to prepare me to again see the spiritual realm, but by this time I'd learned that in Jesus I had authority over the devil and his power, and I'd learned *how* to use my authority.

"It's been fifteen years since my initial introduction to the spiritual realm. Today my husband and I have learned to intercede by using our authority over satanic powers.

"At first it seems very difficult to distinguish between an attack of Satan and God's allowing certain things in our lives. Over the years we have learned it is best to make sure the enemy has no stronghold in the situation. Our response to most situations is to bind Satan and every demon and every work or power of darkness, and to continue to do so until the matter is resolved. At the same time we ask God to bring his perfect plan into the situation. We find appropriate Scriptures, memorize them, and speak them aloud concerning our lives and the lives of others.

"If the situation persists, we realize that God is using a circumstance to bring us to deeper maturity and to change our character. At this point we begin to self-examine, to try to cooperate with the Holy Spirit to make changes he desires to see in us."

## INSTILLING FEAR

Yet another woman shared how she became aware of the enemy's attack against her and how she learned to resist:

"I was a new bride living in an unfamiliar city. My husband traveled extensively. Satan used my loneliness as a means of instilling fear. He subjected me to a series of noises.

"For several months, whenever my husband was out of town, I'd be awakened in the night by the sound of my husband's voice and noises he would make while working in his office. I could hear drawers opening and closing and the computer clicking. Although I was wide awake, the sounds would continue for some time and in great detail. I was greatly troubled by it.

"After several months of such occurrences, I was led by the Lord to come directly against the devil's schemes in the name of Jesus Christ. As I did this repeatedly, the noises stopped and never recurred. I received a great deal of strength and confidence, and my fear was replaced by well-directed anger at the devil. I learned that persistent prayer renders Satan powerless, and his attack cannot continue."

As these stories illustrate, it is critical that we learn to discern between God's dealings *with* us and the devil's attack *against* us. The next time you feel as if a ton of bricks has fallen on your head, you may want to ask, "God, is this a temptation, a test, or an attack?" We desire to pass God's tests, to resist temptation, and to fight any satanic attack.

### Speak, Lord

"Father, just as Jesus prayed that you would protect his disciples from the evil one, we ask that you also protect us. Teach us to clearly hear your voice and see your plan, your direction. Teach us how to discern when we are under attack by the devil and how to use our weapons effectively.

"We love you, Lord, and our greatest desire is to serve you and to please you. Speak to our hearts, Lord, for your servants are listening."

# THIRTEEN

# Lessons from the Field

*No weapon that is formed against you shall prosper, and every tongue that shall rise against you in judgment you shall show to be in the wrong. This is the heritage of the servants of the Lord. This is the righteousness or the vindication which they obtain from me, says the Lord.*

**Isaiah 54:17, *TAB***

W OMEN FACE PROBLEMS unique to women. Here we share lessons from the field—stories of women who faced problems like some of you are facing now or may confront in the future.

## IN THE WORKPLACE

Both single and married women juggle work and family and other interests to contribute their share as breadwinners. Finding the right job isn't always easy either. But as Eunice learned, even when the job doesn't seem right at first, it may be exactly where God wants you.

With her children all enrolled in school, Eunice decided to return to her nursing career. She asked the Lord for a job where she could pray with patients who might be ready to receive him. If she accepted the job she wanted, on the cancer floor of the university hospital, her bosses would be the chief of the oncology unit and the head nurse, with whom he was having an affair. Both were known to be anti-Christian. Should she take this job, knowing it would involve tests and trials?

At her interview Eunice asked the doctor point-blank, "Can I pray with patients?" "Aw, go ahead," he snarled. "I need you here immediately, so you're hired."

As Eunice went on her nursing rounds, she prayed for any patient who wanted prayer. But working with a doctor and head nurse who mocked her God was a challenge. She often overheard them swearing and making fun of her for actually believing that prayer could help anybody on a cancer ward. She didn't argue with them; she just called on the Lord for strength to keep at it.

One day when Eunice felt she'd really been targeted for abuse, she heard the Lord whisper, "Don't let Satan remove you from where I've placed you and called you to stand." After that she determined not to give up. And she kept praying.

A year later the chief of the department and his head nurse were fired. Gradually, many other godless people were removed. Most were replaced by believers. Today, some nine years later, it's not unusual for several nurses to meet with Eunice in the supply room, their "prayer closet." They openly talk to the patients about their Christian faith and have seen many come to know the Lord.

"It was anything but easy those first months," Eunice said.

"The enemy wanted me to throw in the towel, but God wanted someone who could bring his life to the patients. I'm glad he helped me stick it out."

## "LORD, LOVE THROUGH ME"

Denise faced a wrenching decision when her homosexual son asked if he and his companion could move into the cottage behind her home. Both were too sick with AIDS to work.

Together Denise and her husband sought God's answer. Yes, they finally decided, Dean and his friend could come. "I do not approve of homosexuality; it is a sin," she says. "On the other hand, God told me he'd use me to help homosexuals if I could just let him love them through me."

Two-and-a-half years after Denise let Dean and his friend move in, she was able to make this "Hallelujah list" of what God had done through her obedience:

- Dean's companion accepted Jesus.
- Dean is responding to her unconditional love ("Mom, I need a hug today"), though he hasn't yet made Jesus Lord of his life.
- Denise has learned a new depth of intercessory prayer and spiritual warfare through her own personal crisis—and she's now teaching these principles to others.
- She plans to start a Christian support group for women with AIDS, at the invitation of the county task force where she lives.
- She shares one-on-one with mothers whose children have AIDS.
- She now teaches a Bible study in her home.

While Denise still abhors the sin of homosexual behavior, she continually asks God to help her keep her own attitudes Christ-like.

"Jeremiah sat where sinners sat, and God's asked me to do that too," she said. "I also have to face the fact that my son might die soon. But my greatest struggle is when my husband and I come against the demonic forces holding our son back from receiving Jesus and being set free from sin. Dean says Christianity is fine for us, but he prefers his gay activist groups. That really hurts. My part is to extend love to him, but also to do warfare and pray behind the scenes."

## DERISION BECOMES COMPASSION

Another mom with a son in the gay world says her situation has caused her to look at homosexuals in a completely different light: as a challenge for prayer and warfare. She writes: "My heart has been broken for my only child. But I also weep for other young people—many from Christian homes—who are trapped in Satan's cruel deception. I can't see a 'gay' person on the street or in a store without thinking, 'I wonder if anyone is praying for him?'

"One time an acquaintance, who doesn't know about my son, commented about a homosexual working at the hair salon she goes to. 'I don't want him to even touch me,' she said with a shudder. I can't imagine Jesus ever making such a remark. Suppose the woman caught in adultery (Jn 8:3) had been a male homosexual prostitute? Would Jesus have encouraged the crowd to stone the man? I think many in the church today would have.

"I used to be incensed about the gay activists I read about in the newspaper. Then the Lord told me to start praying for them, as well as their families. I found out that the president of the gay activist group in our city was the son of a Pentecostal pastor, and the leader who succeeded him was the son of an Evangelical pastor. Both young men have since died of AIDS. As I prayed for them, God replaced my derision with compassion for them and their families. How can we hope to win them if we treat them like lepers?"

## A WIDOW OVERCOMES GRIEF

Whenever he can, the enemy uses grief to paralyze a woman's emotions and nullify her Christian witness. If there was ever a woman who could have given in to her deep sorrow, it was Emily.

She was twenty-seven when her test-pilot husband was killed during World War II. Crushed with grief, she blamed God for leaving her a widow with a four-year-old. Her mother told her, "Emily, Jesus is a Good Shepherd, and you are one of his little lambs. He'll take care of you. Just trust him."

Emily's anger toward God lifted as she began to study the Word of God. She discovered that the Shepherd really did love her.

After returning to college, she began designing children's clothes. Six years later she met a lawyer who proposed marriage.

"I knew I didn't love him like my first love, but by now I had grown in the Lord and could love him with God's love,"

Emily shared. "So I married him. He was a kind, gentle man. But after we'd had sixteen years together, he died of a heart condition. Again I found myself a widow."

The Lord gave Emily a verse that helped her through her second bout of grief: "No one who puts his hand to the plow and looks back is fit for service in the kingdom of God" (Lk 9:62).

Emily has been a widow now for twenty years, and God has been a faithful husband to her as she presses closer and closer to him. She says, "I don't look back, because if I did I would not accomplish what God has for me to do for him today." What she does for him is head up the intercessory group at her large urban church.

Her advice for other widows:

- Don't let bitterness, anger, or grief rob you of a fulfilled life today. Release those feelings to God.
- Thank God for the spouse you had and for the good years you enjoyed together. Be grateful.
- Trust the Lord to meet your needs in the areas where you once depended on a husband.
- Read the Word of God, study it, and get to know the Lord personally.
- Reach out to others, especially to other widows, and help bring healing into their lives.

## A STRANGE CURSE

Betty, who serves on her church's counseling and deliverance team, was puzzled when her son developed a strange physical problem that didn't respond to medical care or prayer.

Her son Steve was in high school when he began having boils under his arms. After many prescriptions and weekly doctor visits, the physician lanced the boils. But they wouldn't heal. Steve went to the doctor daily to get the wounds cauterized. Then he got a staph infection, requiring a hospital stay and more treatments. After almost three years, sweat glands from under both arms were removed. But healing still eluded him.

One day while Betty was cleaning Steve's room, she found an old folded-up sheet of paper Steve had taken out of his wallet that morning. Printed on it was an Arabian curse that read: "Because you parked in my place, may the fleas of a thousand camels infest your armpits."

Betty couldn't believe it. Could Steve's infirmity possibly be the result of a curse? In the past three years she'd fasted, prayed, and anointed Steve with oil for his healing.

"I never suspected Steve could be the victim of a curse," she said, "if you could call those ridiculous words on a scrap paper a curse. But he had carried it in his wallet for three years, and for three years he'd had this problem. It was weird!"

That afternoon when he got home from school, Steve and Betty destroyed the note and audibly declared in the name of Jesus the curse was broken, along with any power that might be affecting Steve's physical problem.

Steve's healing came amazingly quickly, and never again was he bothered with irritation under his arms.

PRAYING WITH DISCERNMENT

Janet's six-year-old son Kevin came in from school one day with a defiant, sassy attitude.

"What did you do in school today, Son?" Janet asked, puzzled by his mood.

"Played with a crystal ball the teacher brought. We asked it all kinds of questions," he answered.

"Lord, what shall I do about this?" Janet, a new Christian, prayed silently. From deep within she heard, "Break the witchcraft and curses that come with it."

"Kevin, come sit on my lap for a minute," she said, still asking the Lord *how* to follow the directions she'd just received. She gave Kevin a big hug as he climbed on her lap. Surprised, she heard herself saying, "Father, in the name of Jesus I break the power of witchcraft and curses, and I take back from the enemy the ground he has stolen from my son. We give that ground back to you, Lord. Thank you for your protection and your blessing upon Kevin."

After prayer, Kevin immediately changed back to her happy, sweet-natured kid. "That was my introduction to dealing with invisible evil forces," Janet said. "In a nutshell, I quickly learned about spiritual warfare, and I'm still using it for both of my children."

Kevin is grown now, and drives a huge cattle transport trailer-truck across the country. One night Janet woke up four times, and each time she "saw" a truck going off the road. The truck was the eighteen-wheeler Kevin was driving.

"I began binding the spirits of death and calamity, then I asked the Lord to send angels to keep my son's truck on the road. I did it four times that night," she remembers.

At dawn Kevin called to say, "Mom, I'm back in town, but I'm too tired to drive home. Four times last night my truck almost went off the road. Were you praying?"

We need to be alert, sensitive to the Holy Spirit's nudging day and night, and available to do warfare and pray at a moment's notice.

## COMPROMISING VOWS

Sometimes women open themselves to oppression from the enemy when they take oaths in joining secret societies. During Rae's first weeks at college, she was thrilled when a social club invited her to join. Against the advice of her pastor and parents, she accepted, paid her dues, and made a pledge. But the more she attended the meetings and got into the swing of this group's life, the more frequent her headaches and depression became.

In prayer one day she asked the Lord to show her the root cause. "You took vows inconsistent with your Christian faith," was the answer she heard.

She repented and asked God's forgiveness. She then tried to get out of her commitment, only to be told she couldn't do it. She called the national headquarters and demanded that her name be removed from the membership list.

"I was set free—of guilt, depression, and headaches—because I knew I should never have joined that organization in the first place," she reported.

Rae cancelled her vows by having her name removed from the club's membership. Others get rid of a ring or pin that symbolizes their vows, or they renounce in prayer their association with any secret organization that compromises their commitment to Christ.

## A SPIRIT OF BITTERNESS

Any difficulty we or a family member faces in life gives us an opportunity to seek God's battle plan for resolving it.

Ginger was more than concerned because her daughter Chris, a dedicated Christian, was in conflict with her college roommate. The girls had been close friends in high school and had looked forward to rooming together. But arguments and disagreements were too common.

One weekend when Ginger stayed overnight in the dorm with Chris while the roommate was away, she discovered two disturbing facts. First, the previous year a race riot had exploded in that very dorm room, leaving some students with bloody noses. Secondly, Chris's roommate had made a cross-stitched plaque and hung it over their door: "Dorm Bitter Dorm." It was a take-off on "Home Sweet Home."

"It seemed the room had been invaded with spirits of anger, hate, wrath, rage, resentment, and murder—spirits that had been 'invited' through rioting the previous semester," Ginger said. "And the sign above the door didn't help matters: it was like putting out a welcome mat for a spirit of bitterness.

"Chris and I removed the sign. Then using Jesus' name and authority, we told the unclean spirits to leave that dorm room. Chris asked the Lord to forgive her for her part in the strife with her roommate. Then we asked God to fill the room with his peace.

"The results were almost immediate," Ginger said. "It seemed the air had been cleansed and a blanket of peace pervaded the room. The girls are no longer roommates, but they remain friends."

## A SPIRIT OF LUST

While Ginger saw a cross-stitched plaque invite a spirit of bitterness into a place, Katherine found out that evil spirits sometimes attach themselves to ungodly objects.

A Christian speaker who travels extensively, Katherine was staying in the home of a woman she'd never met. As she put her suitcase in the guest room closet, she was overwhelmed with lustful thoughts and feelings. She rebuked the thoughts and commanded that any evil spirits leave the room. She even called her husband and asked him to pray for her. The thoughts left.

That evening Katherine opened the closet to hang up her clothes, and once again she was bombarded with lustful thoughts. When she pulled the string on the closet light and let go of it suddenly, it flipped onto the top shelf of the closet. Reaching up to retrieve it, she found a couple of magazines lying there. She pulled them down and was shocked to see they were blatantly pornographic.

Now Katherine understood why a spirit of lust seemed to attack her mind when she opened the closet. She asked her hostess to come see what she'd discovered and she confided she too had experienced lustful feelings whenever she cleaned that closet.

The woman confronted her nineteen-year-old son, and he

admitted this was his secret hiding place for his porn magazines. With the issue out in the open, he agreed to counseling.

"Since then," Katherine said, "whenever I stay in a hotel or guest room, I make it a habit to command every unclean spirit that might be present to leave in the name and authority of Jesus Christ. All kinds of spirits dwell in hotel rooms where illicit sex, drug dealing, perversion, and porn movies have been going on."

## PROVIDING PRAYER COVER

People who travel in ministry as Katherine does are keenly aware of their need for prayer cover as they work on the front lines of confrontation with the enemy. A young woman missionary, after her first term of service in Southeast Asia, wrote in her newsletter:

If folks at home don't pray for me, then I'd better stay at home! My reaction to my first term of service is that the mission field is like a fierce battlefield, in which there are no cease-fires. In an ordinary war, ground soldiers are not expected to fight unless sufficient air cover is provided; otherwise they might soon be wiped out.

Constant overhead protection and reinforcements are vital. Any country sending troops into ground battle without such support might justly be accused of condemning these men to defeat and death.

Similarly, it seems to me to be equally irresponsible for a church to send someone out as its representative into the

warfare of the mission field, if that church is unable or unwilling to maintain sufficient, continual praying forces to
defeat the enemy attacks that strike missionaries continually.[1]

While this account is from a missionary's point of view,
the need for "prayer cover" applies in many situations: a
husband or family member working in dangerous surroundings, a child at camp or college or living in a city like New
York, a Christian teacher trying to uphold godly standards in
a public school classroom. The list goes on.

## ARE YOU ENLISTED?

In this book we've discussed a lot of problems and challenges facing women today. The question remains: *Where are
the Deborahs and Esthers of our generation?*

The Deborahs are those who will get God's instructions
and go to war against the enemy, confident that God goes
before them.

The Esthers are those who will intercede before the King
on behalf of their people, those born for such a time as this
who will pay the price to get a wicked proclamation re-
versed.

Nancy Clarke writes in Women's Aglow *Connection:*

We Christians are the people of God, empowered by
him to defeat Satan's forces and the stronghold they have
in the minds and hearts of men. God depends on us to de-
liver the power blow so that, as we reach out to hurting

people in our communities, they will be open to hear his message. God has an army forming to help open the way in the midst of the war zones in which we live. Time is wasting. Join up now."[2]

How true this is of spiritual warfare! Our liberation began with Jesus' death, burial, and resurrection. Satan has no legal power over us, although he continues to wreak havoc in the world. Our Savior, the seed of the woman, crushed his head and broke his power. Now it's up to us to exert the authority Jesus invested in us to take back the ground the enemy has stolen. We have nothing to fear!

Because we are God's children, "He who lives in us is greater than he who is in the world" (1 Jn 4:4, TAB).

The women who proclaim the good news are a great army.

# Epilogue

I LOVE TO READ BIBLE STORIES of how God uses women to accomplish something for him—regardless of how insignificant they may seem to others.

Miriam, Moses' sister, leads the women in a celebration song and dance when the Pharaoh's chariots with their horsemen are thrown into the sea.

A Hebrew slave in the household of Syria's army commander, Naaman, sends him to the prophet Elisha for healing of his leprosy. One woman interceding.

With the promise to dedicate him to the Lord, Hannah begs God for a son, then indeed releases her boy Samuel to train in the temple and become a prophet.

Ordinary women like you and me. The New Testament tells about a lot of them. Martha serves Jesus meals, while Mary sits at his feet. Women minister to Jesus with their money and talents. The Samaritan woman at the well has just one encounter with Jesus, then runs to tell all her village about the Messiah. Women are last at the cross and first at the tomb, then are the first to proclaim the good news, "He is risen!" Dorcas, a woman disciple, is so full of good deeds that Peter raises her from the dead so she can continue her work. And the list goes on.

Whenever I wonder whether my prayers or ministry

make any difference, I reread these wonderful stories of women whom God used and whose prayers he heard. And I realize once again that God has gifted each of us with a unique call and talent.

Now, more than ever, women must intercede that their family members may accomplish God's plan and purpose for them. Recently an evangelist said, "We are at a moment in time when there are few mothers and fathers in Zion who will stand in the prayer gap for the coming new generation of young soldiers of the cross."

I want to challenge all believing women to become prayer warriors for this "Joshua generation"—the young who are going in to possess the land for Jesus Christ, much as Joshua went into the Promised Land after Moses' death. This young army of volunteers includes warriors like Keith, Dana, Quinett, Kim, Sherry, David, Greg, Larry, Daniel, Christopher, Wendy, Tracey, Linda, Marcus, Gordon, Kathy, Cindy, Mike, Becky, Eugene, and Christin.

There is a war raging—one that we cannot see with our eyes, but just as real and even more destructive than wars among nations. This is a war for souls, a war of eternal consequences.

We are authorized by Jesus and empowered by the Holy Spirit to do battle. With our orders from God's Word, we Christian women must take our positions in God's army. Let's learn how to pray more effectively and how to fight in the spiritual realm until those we love are truly liberated in Jesus.

God is calling modern-day Deborahs into the prayer

closet for battle. I pray this book has inspired and challenged you to be among the warriors whose hope is anchored in the unshakable power of God!

—Quin Sherrer

# Notes

## ONE
### But I Never Wanted to Be in a Battle!

1. C.S. Lewis, *The Screwtape Letters*, (New York: Macmillan, 1961), p. 3.
2. Dr. Herbert Lockyer, *All the Women of the Bible*, (Grand Rapids, MI: Zondervan Books, 1958), p. 41.

## TWO
### Who Is the Enemy? And What Does He Want from Me?

1. R. Arthur Mathews, *Born for Battle*, (Robesonia, PA: OMF Books, 1978), pp. 31, 32.
2. Dean Sherman, *Spiritual Warfare for Every Christian*, (Seattle, WA: Frontline Communications, 1990), p. 82.
3. Sherman, pp. 83, 84.
4. McCandlish Phillips, *The Bible, the Supernatural, and the Jews*, (New York: World Publishing Co., 1970), p. 73.
5. Edith Schaeffer, *A Way of Seeing*, (Old Tappan, NJ: Fleming H. Revell Co., 1977), p. 110.
6. Richard D. Dobbins, "Caring for the Casualties," *Charisma* magazine, (Lake Mary, FL: Strang Communications, September 1990), p. 96.
7. William Gurnall, *The Christian in Complete Armour*, Vol. 1, abridged by Ruthanne Garlock, et.al. (Edinburgh, Scotland and Carlisle, PA: Banner of Truth Trust, 1986), p. 54.

### THREE
### What Our Spiritual Wardrobe Should Look Like

1. Gurnall, Vol. 1, pp. 66, 68.
2. Gurnall, Vol. 2, pp. 22, 23.
3. W.E. Vine, *Vine's Expository Dictionary of Old and New Testament Words*, Vol. 3 (Old Tappan, NJ: Fleming H. Revell, 1981), pp. 298, 299.
4. Gurnall, Vol. 1, p. 29.
5. Gurnall, Vol. 2, pp. 149, 160.
6. Gurnall, Vol. 2, pp. 386, 388.
7. Gurnall, Vol. 3, pp. 27, 28, 30, 31.
8. Gurnall, Vol. 1, p. 48.
9. Sherman, p. 45.
10. Vine, Vol. 4, p. 230.
11. Mathews, p. 17.
12. Mathews, p. 22.
13. Gurnall, Vol. 3, p. 164.

### FOUR
### How Strong Can a Woman Be?

1. Associated Press article, "Study: Moms Credited Most in Instilling Faith," (statistics by Search Institute of Minneapolis), Fort Walton, Florida *Daily News*, February 10, 1990.
2. John Dawson, *Taking Our Cities for God*, (Lake Mary, FL: Creation House, 1989), pp. 27, 28, 29.
3. Dawson, p. 189.
4. Judson Cornwall, *Praying the Scriptures*, (Lake Mary, FL: Creation House, 1990), pp. 212, 213.

### FIVE
### The Disciplines of the Spirit-Empowered Woman

1. Finis Jennings Dake, *Dake's Annotated Reference Bible*, (Lawrenceville, GA: Dake Bible Sales, Inc., 1963), p. 629, New Testament section. [Other references given by Dake: Psalm 35:13 and 69:10; 2 Samuel 12:16-23; Ezra 8:21;

Matthew 4:1-11, 6:16-18, 9:15; Luke 5:33; Acts 9:7-9, 13:1-5; 1 Corinthians 7:5.]

2. Arthur Wallis, *God's Chosen Fast*, (Fort Washington, PA: Christian Literature Crusade, 1968), pp. 41, 42, 86.

3. Gloria Phillips with Irene Burke Harrell, *A Heart Set Free*, (Wilson, NC: Star Books, 1985), pp. 39-41.

SIX

*Our Weapons and Strategy*

1. Paul E. Billheimer, *Destined to Overcome*, (Minneapolis, MN: Bethany House, 1982), pp. 41, 43.

2. Sherman, p. 123.

3. H.A. Maxwell Whyte, *The Power of the Blood*, (Springdale, PA: Whitaker House, 1973), p. 44.

4. Whyte, pp. 78, 80, 81.

5. Mathews, p. 66.

6. Mathews, p. 124.

7. Linda Raney Wright, *Spiritual Warfare and Evangelism*, (Crestline, CA: Linda Raney Wright), p. 9.

SEVEN

*An Open Door to the Enemy*

1. *The E. W. Bullinger Companion Bible*, (Grand Rapids, MI: Zondervan, 1964), appendix 44.iv.

2. Burton Stokes and Lynn Lucas, *No Longer a Victim*, (Shippensburg, PA: Destiny Image Publishers, 1988), p. 25.

3. Derek Prince, *Blessing or Curse*, (Old Tappan, NJ: Chosen Books, 1990), pp. 19, 145.

4. Phillips, pp. 75, 76.

5. Herbert Lockyer, Sr., editor, *Nelson's Illustrated Bible Dictionary*, (Nashville, TN: Thomas Nelson, 1986), p. 501.

6. Ed Murphy, "We Are at War" in book *Wrestling with Dark Angels*, edited by C. Peter Wagner and F. Douglas Pennoyer (Ventura, CA: Regal Books, 1990), p. 60.

7. Murphy, p. 58.
8. Murphy, pp. 68-71.

EIGHT
Breaking Bondages

1. We deal with this subject in more detail in our two previous books, *How to Forgive Your Children*, (Aglow) and *How to Pray for Your Family and Friends*, (Servant).
2. Dr. Archibald D. Hart, *Healing Life's Hidden Addictions*, (Ann Arbor, MI: Servant Publications, 1990), p. 238.
3. We recommend Jan Frank's book, *A Door of Hope*, (Here's Life Publishers, Inc., P. O. Box 1576, San Bernardino, CA 92402, 1987). Here's Life Publishers can refer you to Christian incest counseling centers in many cities of the U.S.
4. Anonymous, "One Woman's Walk through an Abortion Nightmare," *Charisma* magazine, October 1990, p. 96. Used by permission of the author.
5. "One Woman's Walk through an Abortion Nightmare," p. 106.
6. "One Woman's Walk through an Abortion Nightmare," pp. 106, 107.
7. "One Woman's Walk through an Abortion Nightmare," p. 108.

NINE
Fight for Your Children

1. Johanna Michaelson, *Like Lambs to the Slaughter*, (Eugene, OR: Harvest House Publishers, 1989), pp. 11, 13.
2. Mel Gabler, "Have You Read Your Child's School Textbooks?" pamphlet published by Educational Research Analysts, P. O. Box 7518, Longview, TX 75601.
3. Mel Gabler, Educational Research Analysts Newsletter, June 1990, p. 3.
4. Deborah Mendenhall, "Nightmarish Textbooks Await Your

Kids," *Citizen* magazine, published by Focus on the Family, P.O. Box 500, Pomona, CA 91769, September 17, 1990, pp. 4, 5.

5. Greg Reid, *Teen Satanism: Redeeming the Devil's Children*, (Columbus, GA: Quill Publications, 1990) p. 6. Greg Reid's ministry organization is Youthfire, P.O. Box 370006, El Paso, TX 79936, (915) 595-3569.

6. Reid, p. 13.

7. Reid, p. 14.

8. Reid, p. 15.

9. Reid, p. 9.

10. See guidelines in Quin Sherrer's book, *How to Pray for Your Children*, (Lynnwood, WA: Aglow Publications, 1986).

## TEN
### Fight for Your Marriage

1. *Time* Magazine, Special Issue, Fall 1990, *Women: The Road Ahead*, from article, "What Youth Think," p. 14.

2. Dr. James Dobson, *Love Must Be Tough*, (Waco, TX: Word Books, 1983), pp. 122, 123.

3. Dobson, pp. 71, 72.

4. Dr. Archibald Hart, *Children and Divorce*, (Dallas, TX: Word, Inc., 1982), pp. 34, 35.

5. Hart, p. 50-62.

6. Judy Reamer, *Feelings Women Rarely Share*, (Springdale, PA: Whitaker House, 1987) pp. 89, 92.

7. Reamer, pp. 144, 145.

## ELEVEN
### Spiritual Healing and Warfare

1. Jamie Buckingham, "The Buckingham Report," *Ministries Today*, (Lake Mary, FL: Strang Publishing, Inc., January-February, 1991), p. 21. Used with permission of Jamie Buckingham.

2. Arlene Strackbein, "Battle of the Mind," *Mighty Warrior* newsletter, (San Antonio, TX: Intercessors International, Summer 1989), pp. 6, 7, 9. Used with permission.
3. Johanna Michaelsen, *The Beautiful Side of Evil*, (Eugene, OR: Harvest House Publishers, 1982), from the Foreword by Hal Lindsey.
4. *The Beautiful Side of Evil*, p. 179.
5. *The Beautiful Side of Evil*, p. 192.

THIRTEEN
*Lessons from the Field*

1. Anne J. Townsend, *Prayer without Pretending*, (Chicago, IL: Moody Press, 1973), pp. 45-46.
2. Nancy Clarke, Aglow's *Connection* newsletter, (Edmonds, WA: Women's Aglow Fellowship International, December 1990), p. 6.

# Bibliography of Recommended Reading

**Billheimer, Paul E.**, *Destined to Overcome*, (Minneapolis, MN: Bethany House, 1981).

**Cornwall, Judson**, *Praying the Scriptures*, (Lake Mary, FL: Creation House, 1990).

**Dawson, John**, *Taking Our Cities for God*, (Lake Mary, FL: Creation House, 1989).

**Dobson, Dr. James**, *Love Must Be Tough*, (Waco, TX: Word Books, 1983).

**Frank, Jan**, *A Door of Hope*, (Here's Life Publishers, Inc., P.O. Box 1576, San Bernardino, CA 92402, 1987).

**Gurnall, William**, *The Christian in Complete Armour*, Volumes 1, 2, and 3, abridged by Ruthanne Garlock, et.al. (Edinburgh, Scotland and Carlisle, PA: Banner of Truth Trust, 1986).

**Hart, Dr. Archibald**, *Healing Life's Hidden Addictions*, (Ann Arbor, MI: Servant Publications, 1990).

**Lewis, C.S.**, *The Screwtape Letters* (New York: Macmillan, 1961).

**Marrs, Texe**, *Ravaged by the New Age*, (Austin, TX: Living Truth Publishers, 1989).

**Marrs, Wanda**, *New Age Lies to Women*, (Austin, TX: Living Truth Publishers, 1989).

**Mathews, R. Arthur**, *Born for Battle*, (Robesonia, PA: OMF Books, 1978).

**Michaelson, Johanna**, *Like Lambs to the Slaughter*, (Eugene, OR: Harvest House Publishers, 1989).

**Michaelson, Johanna**, *The Beautiful Side of Evil*, (Eugene, OR: Harvest House Publishers, 1982).

**Phillips, Gloria,** with Irene Burke Harrell, *A Heart Set Free,* (Wilson, NC: Star Books, 1985).

**Phillips, McCandlish,** *The Bible, The Supernatural, and the Jews,* (New York: World Publishing Co., 1970).

**Phillips, Phil,** *Saturday Morning Mind Control,* (Nashville, TN: Oliver Nelson, 1991).

**Prince, Derek,** *Blessing or Curse,* (Old Tappan, NJ: Chosen Books, 1990).

**Reamer, Judy,** *Feelings Women Rarely Share,* (Springdale, PA: Whitaker House, 1987).

**Reid, Greg,** *Teen Satanism: Redeeming the Devil's Children,* (Columbus, GA: Quill Publications, 1990). Available from Youthfire, P.O. Box 370006, El Paso, TX 79936.

**Schaeffer, Edith,** *A Way of Seeing,* (Old Tappan, NJ: Fleming H. Revell Co., 1977).

**Sherman, Dean,** *Spiritual Warfare for Every Christian,* (Seattle, WA: Frontline Communications, 1990).

**Sherrer, Quin,** *How to Pray for Your Children,* (Lynnwood, WA: Aglow Publications, 1986).

**Sherrer, Quin, and Ruthanne Garlock,** *How To Forgive Your Children,* (Lynnwood, WA: Aglow Publications, 1989).

**Sherrer, Quin, and Ruthanne Garlock,** *How To Pray for Your Family and Friends,* (Ann Arbor, MI: Servant Publications, 1990).

**Stokes, Burton, and Lynn Lucas,** *No Longer a Victim,* (Shippensburg, PA: Destiny Image Publishers, 1988).

**Wagner, C. Peter, and F. Douglas Pennoyer,** editors, *Wrestling with Dark Angels,* (Ventura, CA: Regal Books, 1990).

**Wallis, Arthur,** *God's Chosen Fast,* (Fort Washington, PA: Christian Literature Crusade, 1968).

**White, Thomas B.,** *The Believer's Guide to Spiritual Warfare,* (Ann Arbor, MI: Servant Publications, 1990).

**Wright, Linda Raney,** *Spiritual Warfare and Evangelism,* (Crestline, CA: Linda Raney Wright).

# APPENDIX

## ARSENAL SCRIPTURES FOR SPIRITUAL WARFARE

**Why pray:**
Ezekiel 22:30
James 5:16
1 Timothy 2:1-2

**Authority over the enemy:**
Isaiah 44:25, 26a; 54:17; 55:11; 59:19
Jeremiah 1:12
Matthew 10:8; 12:28, 29; 16:19
Mark 3:27; 6:7; 16:17
Luke 10:19
2 Corinthians 2:14
Ephesians 1:19-22; 4:8; 6:10-18
Colossians 2:15
Revelation 1:18

**For strength and declaration of victory:**
1 Samuel 17:45
2 Samuel 22:33, 35, 40
2 Kings 6:16, 17
Psalms 18:29; 68:28; 149:6-9
Song of Solomon 6:10

Isaiah 41:15; 50:7
Jeremiah 12:5; 23:29

**For those in authority:**
Psalm 37:23
Proverbs 21:1
1 Timothy 2:1, 2

**For the nations:**
Joshua 1:3
Psalms 2:8; 68:32-35; 108:1-5
Jeremiah 1:10; 15:19-21; 51:21
Daniel 12:3
Micah 4:13

**For guidance:**
Psalms 34:19; 37:23, 24; 123:1, 2
Proverbs 3:5, 6
Isaiah 30:21
2 Corinthians 5:7

**For peace of mind:**
Deuteronomy 33:27
Psalm 31:24
Isaiah 26:3
John 14:27
1 Corinthians 2:16b
2 Corinthians 10:5
Ephesians 2:14, 15
Philippians 4:7-9

**For protection:**
Deuteronomy 28:6, 7
Isaiah 54:17
Psalms 5:11; 17:7-9; 91:1-7, 10.
Proverbs 2:8

**For restoration and security:**
Joel 2:18-32
Psalms 31:8; 32:7
Proverbs 10:30; 12:3, 21; 18:10

**For healing:**
Exodus 15:26
Psalm 103:3
Proverbs 3:7, 8; 4:20-22
Isaiah 53:5
Matthew 4:23; 9:28, 29; 15:26-28
Luke 9:11
1 Peter 2:24
1 John 3:8
3 John 2

**For dealing with an abusive husband:**
Leviticus 26:3-13
Deuteronomy 8:7-10
2 Chronicles 15:7
Psalms 31:20, 21; 32:7; 91; 144:11; 145:18
Ezekiel 28:24-26

**For sleeplessness:**
Matthew 11:28-30
Job 11:18, 19
Psalms 4:8; 127:2
Proverbs 3:24
Mark 4:37-39

**For provision and finances:**
Deuteronomy 8:18
1 Kings 17:2-4, 8, 9
2 Chronicles 32:8
Proverbs: 3:2; 10:3; 11:23, 25; 12:12; 13:21, 22, 25
Isaiah 54:5

Malachi 3:10, 11
Matthew 6:25, 32
Luke 6:38

**For a new job:**
Deuteronomy 28:3-14; 31:8
Joshua 1:3, 5-9
2 Chronicles 15:7
Psalm 1:3

**For weariness and depression:**
Psalms 28:7-9; 30:11, 12; 55:18
Isaiah 40:28-31; 41:10; 43:2, 18, 19; 45:2, 3

**For children:**
1 Kings 4:29
Psalms 127:3-5; 144:12
Isaiah 11:2; 43:5; 49:25; 54:13; 59:21
Jeremiah 29:11-14; 31:16, 17
Daniel 1:9, 20
Ephesians 1:17; 6:4
Philippians 4:19
Colossians 1:9-12
James 1:2

**For wayward family members:**
Psalm 140:1, 2, 4, 8
Isaiah 59:1
Jeremiah 33:26
2 Corinthians 4:3, 4
2 Timothy 2:25b, 26

**To receive Jesus as Lord:**
John 3:7, 8, 16; 6:37; 10:10b; 14:6
Romans 3:23; 10:9-13
1 John 1:9

## Other Books of Interest by
## Quin Sherrer and Ruthanne Garlock

**The Spiritual Warrior's Prayer Guide**
ISBN 0-89283-809-4
291 pages, $10.99

**Prayers Women Pray: Intimate Moments With God**
ISBN 1-56955-087-5
167 pages, $9.99

**The Making of a Spiritual Warrior**
ISBN 1-56955-111-1
206 pages, $9.99

**Prayer Partnerships**
ISBN 1-56955-254-1
173 pages, $9.99

AVAILABLE AT YOUR LOCAL BOOKSTORE OR
WHEREVER BOOKS ARE SOLD.